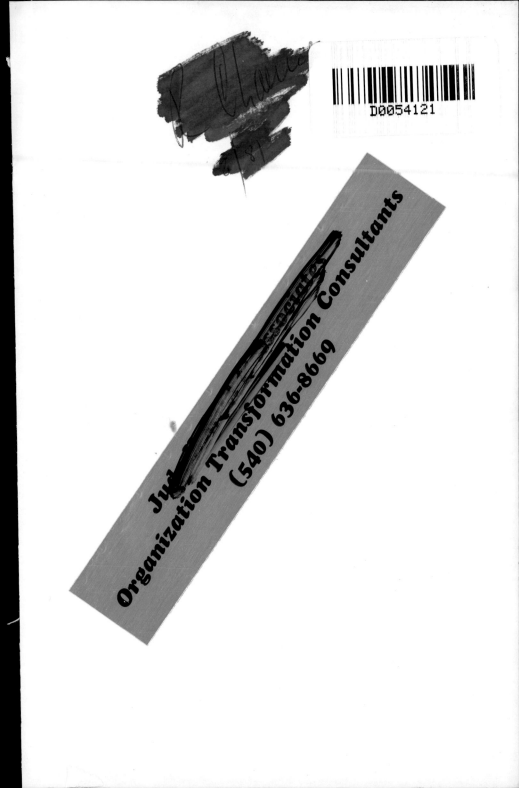

Productivity:
The Human Side

Other Books by the Authors

Synergogy: An Instrumented Team Learning Approach (1981)
The Grid₍ᵣ₎ for Sales Excellence, 2nd ed. (1980)
The Versatile Manager: A Grid Profile (1980)
The New Grid for Supervisory Effectiveness (1978)
The New Managerial Grid (1978)
Consultation (1976)
Diary of an OD Man (1976)
Corporate Excellence Through Grid Organization Development (1968)
The Managerial Grid (1964)

Productivity: The Human Side

A Social Dynamics Approach

Robert R. Blake
and Jane Srygley Mouton

A Division of
American Management Associations

Library of Congress Cataloging in Publication Data

Blake, Robert Rogers, 1918–
    Productivity, the human side.

    Includes index.
    1. Word groups. 2. Labor productivity.
I. Mouton, Jane Srygley. II. Title.
HD66.B53   658.3'14   80-69695
ISBN 0-8144-5692-8   AACR2

First Printing

Preface

The behavioral sciences are a gold mine of ideas about how to be effective in achieving production with and through others. However, the veins in this mine cannot all be mined at once. One of the richest is described here. It is that area within the behavioral sciences that demonstrates how thinking among those who are gathered in small groups tends to converge around norms. Once established, these norms have a regulating effect through group pressures applied to individuals who stray from uniformities of thought and action.

This tendency toward convergence, with its resulting pressures to conform, accounts for many phenomena seen in industrial, government, and other kinds of organizations today. When managers recognize and understand these principles of group behavior, they can lead in such a way as to promote productivity, reduce absenteeism and inferior quality, and stimulate the creativity that is so essential for finding sound solutions to the many chronic and acute problems facing us.

The behavioral science principles described here are not difficult to understand. It is clearly within the scope of any manager to put them to use in order to achieve benefits of the kind described above. The case studies offered in this book present problems that have been resolved successfully through daily application of these principles.

A reservoir of invaluable research that has never been brought into focus for operational use stands behind this text. Much important research bearing on the human side of productivity was conducted in the 50-year period between 1920 and 1970, with the largest concentration in the 1950s and 1960s. Although there has been a continuing stream of research on norms since the mid-1960s, it has been concentrated upon very detailed aspects of social influence and is presented here only when it is of direct pertinence to the larger issue of promoting productivity. Through better understanding and management of the underlying process of how social norms and associated attitudes form, of how, once established, they resist change, and of how managers can bring about productivity improvements without provoking resistance, significant productivity gains can be expected to result.

Robert R. Blake
Jane Srygley Mouton

Contents

1 Approaches to Improving Productivity 1

2 Group Norms and Personal Attitudes 17

3 How Norms Arise 23

4 The Formation of Groups 34

5 The Pressure to Conform 43

6 Maintaining Independence 52

7 Intergroup Relationships 63

8 Changing Norms to Improve Productivity 69

9 The Management of Safety 80

10 Reworking the Union–Management Relationship 88

11 The Last Hour of Work 95

12 Designing a Norm-Shifting Seminar 102

13 Releasing Creativity Within Groups 108

14 Conclusion 118

Index 125

Productivity:
The Human Side

1
Approaches
to Improving Productivity

Nothing in the industrial setting is more important than improving productivity. There are many reasons for this. One is that productivity permits better salaries and wages, and these in turn are the bases for a better standard of living. Beyond that, improved productivity keeps the nation afloat and competitive in the international sphere. The third reason is that productive people are happy people. They are satisfied; they find reward in their own effort, and satisfaction is certainly one of the important ingredients in mental health. There is, of course, always the selfish motivation in the sense that owners and shareholders desire improved productivity because the bottom line is profit, and productivity is one of the basic ways of increasing it.

Given the central role of productivity in the design of our society, it is not surprising that there are so many different approaches toward trying to increase it. Some are practically worthless, while others make a very substantial contribution. A review of the more important ones gives us a clue as to the importance that is attached to making improvements in productivity.

Pay

It has traditionally been presumed that as pay increases, productivity improves as well. This is the whole basis of the piece rate system of remunerating the worker for his or her output. But what was thought to be a simple relationship between pay and productivity is really far more complex than that. It is evident that there are ways of exploiting people with pay in order to advance productivity, and the sweatshop of the 1900s is a classic example. We know that using pay to promote productivity beyond a certain level is no longer regarded as legitimate, and unions stand as testimony to the resentment that workers feel when they are pressured for productivity in the name of pay.

Scientific Management

The first decade of this century saw the advent of a very new approach to increasing productivity. Scientific management was invented by Frederick W. Taylor, and it spawned a new industrial discipline of time and motion study. What it actually involved was the industrial engineer taking the job and rethinking it in order to eliminate unnecessary steps and motions, and then putting it back together in such a way that all the worker's efforts had a direct productivity result.

Scientific management also produced resentments, because workers often saw improved productivity with no further improvement in pay and therefore felt exploited. Nonetheless, it has proved to be a very important approach toward improving productivity and it continues to find adherents.

Selection

The psychological testing movement saw the introduction of the notion that some people are naturally more productive than others. Therefore, if the best workers could be spotted in advance by interviews and test results, productivity could be enhanced by selecting them for employment. Although psychological tests can help in some respects, their value is limited, and they too are resented because of the discrimination that results simply because some people are better prepared test-takers than others by virtue of education.

Worker Training

Another idea that has proved to have some inherent value in stimulating productivity, particularly among the newly employed, is training. The idea is that a worker who has been helped to learn the ropes quickly will become more productive in a shorter period of time, and the benefits from doing so are substantial. This is true not only for the new employee; it is equally true for the employee who shifts from one level of job complexity to another. But training, too, has not always been greeted with enthusiasm. Many people fear that they are not rapid learners, and therefore the training will expose them to embarrassment. There are other reasons why people resist training, but the fear of embarrassment is certainly one of the most important ones.

Supervision

The assumption exists that the supervisor is the key to promoting increased output. That is, if a supervisor understands the task at hand and has a good attitude toward subordinates, then the supervisor can deal with them in a better manner. In this way he or she gains their loyalty and stimulates them to be more productive. Supervisory training certainly has made a contribution to working better with and through people to increase productivity, but it also has had the effect of lowering productivity. Some supervisors get the humanistic message that it is good to be nice to people and turn a blind eye to actual losses in productivity. This may be a by-product of their efforts to be pleasant and highly regarded.

Motivation

Motivation has always been recognized as an important factor in productivity. It operates in two ways.

Fear

It is possible to motivate by fear. That means letting people know that it is production or else. Fear was one of the dominant motivators a century ago, but unions were organized to protect people from threats and to create conditions under which a person who is treated unfairly can file a grievance. The welfare state has also had the effect of reducing the fear of unemployment, therefore making it more difficult for managers or supervisors to use threat as the means for promoting productivity.

Rah-rah

As motivation by fear has lessened, rah-rah motivation has become more popular. It is believed that productivity is advanced by generating enthusiasm. This is done by telling people, in an emotional way, how important it is to "win," and the way to win is to do better today than yesterday and better this year than last. Rah-rah motivation can have a beneficial effect in terms of stirring up a lethargic work force, but it is widely recognized that rah-rah motivation quickly dissipates and has to be restimulated.

Participation

The notion of participation was brought into focus in the 1930s. The idea is that the more involved people are in the challenges of production, the more productive they will be. A supervisor does not tell workers what to do, nor ask them to do it; rather, the supervisor gets them to participate. Then they become caught up with being more productive by their own involvement. There are four approaches.

Job Redesign

One of these involves redesigning jobs. Formerly this was called job enlargement, then it was called job enrichment, and now it is referred to as job redesign. They are all the same. The idea is that a person who is involved in rethinking his or her job and what it contains is very likely, particularly with professional help, to want to expand it by taking on more horizontal and vertical activities and being responsible for them. This tends to increase the complexity of work in both directions. Once complexity is increased, the job requires more thought and involvement; therefore one person is contributing more output under the redesigned job than previously.

MBO

MBO has become a part of our national language. It means management by objectives. The idea is that when a person sets objectives, that person becomes involved in demonstrating an ability to accomplish these objectives. The result, of course, is greater productivity.

Many people find that the benefits from a management-by-objectives program are positive but short term. The approach succeeds at first, but then, when achieving the objective becomes dulled by repetition, work tends to return to the old level.

Quality of Work Life (QWL)

This approach to better productivity through worker participation has been emerging in the past few years. If workers are involved more directly in the challenges of production, they will respond with ideas and efforts that improve productivity. This is "direct" participation, often with the formal supervisory system replaced by QWL specialists who lead discussions, act as communications channels to higher levels of management, and so on.

Quality Circles (QC)

This practice is copied from the Japanese. A number of employees are brought together and a discussion is held on how to improve the quantity and quality of production. The underlying principle is that those who do the work have many ideas about how to do it better, and if they are listened to, and if what they recommend is implemented, then improved productivity will result.

These ideas are logical, but there are many limitations inherent in both the quality of work life and quality circle approaches, particularly when employees already have a negative attitude toward management and the company. Many discussions are gripe sessions, not sessions in which constructive thinking is done about how to advance productivity. Beyond that, many employees wait for implementation of suggestions that may not be practical, given the cost and the budget available for them. When nothing happens, the old attitudes reappear, often expressed by "See, we told them, but they don't give a damn. Why should we try to be productive when they don't care?"

The basic notion of having employees participate in thinking about how to increase the quality and quantity of productivity is sound; the way of bringing it into use is what produces resentment and resistance to further efforts if and when recommendations for change fail to materialize.

Sociotechnical Systems

Every job is a combination of two considerations. One is the best technical system for being productive; the other is the best social organization for bringing human resources to bear on that technology. This has become known as the sociotechnical approach. It has been found that when employees are involved in rethinking the social side as well as the technical side of production, they often find better ways of organizing themselves in order to gain the benefits of bringing a positive social system to bear on output.

Of undoubted importance is better equipment. One person with good equipment can be much more productive than a number of people operating with antiquated equipment. When the cost of the advanced equipment is calculated against the improved productivity, it often turns out that better equipment is one of the most effective solutions to the productivity problem. Many observers feel that skill in designing equipment has now advanced to the point where the decade ahead of us will see a rapid expansion of robot technology in which the human contribution to productivity will be eliminated except for maintenance.

In many respects hardware is the ideal solution wherever it can be applied, because people are then not called upon to do the kinds of activities that machinery is capable of doing as well or better. In other words, equipment reduces the dehumanization of work.

Supervisory Norms

Almost invisible and unrecognized but of signal importance is the fact that supervisors, even though they may never meet as a group, do in reality constitute a group. By virtue of being group members they share norms of supervisory behavior and conduct. If these norms are pro-productivity, supervisors will act in such a way as to increase the output of those with and through whom they achieve results. If the supervisory group's norms toward productivity are low, absent, or negative, supervisors will not act with and through the people for whom they are responsible in such a way as to promote output.

Because this is an uncommon way of conceiving the productivity problem, it may be helpful to discuss it in some detail.

Every day we observe people being far less productive than they can be. We see waste, inferior products, and people chatting about matters that have no bearing on their output. Yet sometimes we see the opposite: people applying themselves with enthusiastic effort. We see high output with lean manning, and we see other manifestations of excellent management. What makes the difference?

There are many explanations. Some say that unproductive people lack goals; that those who are committed share a dedicated sense of purpose. Others blame bosses for having an adverse effect on productivity. Still others say bosses use their power and authority to promote excellence. Some point to the workers themselves and say that they are "just an unenthusiastic bunch," while others claim that those who apply themselves are "just naturally enthusiastic."

The operation of a word processing center provides a good example of supervisory norms. This is a relatively new idea. What it involves is a number of people who are competent in typing and editing as well as composing letters. There are several supervisors. The supervisors come to share a norm related to the 24-hour turnaround of correspondence. The elapsed time from receipt of a letter from its author to its return in perfect shape for transmittal should be no longer than 24 hours. Compare this with another word processing center where the several supervisors never come to share an agreement on the maximum time that should be taken in turning correspondence around. The technical competence of both the operators and the supervisors is comparable. The only difference is that in one there exists a shared agreement on a norm that constitutes a very significant challenge to the effectiveness of production; in the other, such a norm never emerges. Which of these would you expect to achieve the higher rate of productivity?

We can take the example another step. A manager says to a supervisor, "This is an emergency letter—I need to send it within 24 hours." The supervisor is in the situation where no norm exists. Now the first time, such a request might be regarded as a special case, and the supervisor will make a special effort to comply. But if the request is repeated, those who operate the word processing center may soon come to feel that an unfair pressure is being applied to them, and they will therefore come to resent such requests. Now the operators of the word processing center criticize the supervisor, who keeps applying pressure for a fast turnaround, and they soon make invidious comparisons among different supervisors—some are spoken of as slavedrivers, while others are thought to be reasonable. Soon the "slavedriver" comes to realize that he or she is generating resentment and has become the target of ridicule. That supervisor is no longer responsive to requests for 24-hour turnaround, but rather prefers either to resist or to promise and fail to deliver in preference to behaving in a way that generates resistance and resentment.

The same request made of a supervisor who is in a section

where 24-hour turnaround is carried out in a mutually supportive way is seen as a matter of routine. If the request were to put undue pressure on one supervisor, the load would be shared among all in the group in order to accomplish the result. That response to such a request is not related to skills of supervision in the more conventional meaning of the term. Instead it involves getting supervisors to develop a shared commitment among themselves to high productivity norms, and it requires promoting the kind of social support that can bring this about.

The opposite is all too often the case. Management pressures for results. Supervisors know they will be criticized by operators if they ask for more production than has been characteristic of the past. Supervisors also expect to be pinned for "brown-nosing" or "bucking for promotion"; therefore they prefer to avoid taking the action that would stimulate productivity in preference to being accepted by others, supervisors and operators alike. As a result, the supervisor becomes skillful at doubletalk.

Some examples may be useful in making more concrete the issue of norms and how they affect productivity. The three problems presented here will be examined in detail as case studies in Chapters 9, 10, and 11.

Example 1   Slacking Off

Employees in one plant have fallen into the habit of slacking off during the last hour of work. Supervisors are aware of this and are under a good deal of pressure from their managers to do something about it. Privately they acknowledge it is a real problem, but in fact they do nothing. Rather, they schedule themselves into their offices during the last hour of the day under the guise of using that hour for planning the next day's work. The result is that they don't have to see the problem. The slacking off has been in existence for three years and is now chronic.

This problem should be corrected, not only because it reflects poor management, but also because it has a serious adverse impact on productivity. Even morale seems to be affected when people line up in front of the clock. Is this a problem between and among supervisors or not? What steps would you take to resolve it?

Example 2   Poor Safety Record

The plant in question is one of 12. It has the worst record in terms of time lost because of accidents. Lost-time accidents have an adverse impact on productivity. The vice-president of manufacturing has focused attention on this problem and has reviewed the accident reports with the plant manager and with the person responsible for safety. The conclusion is that almost all the accidents, close to 98 percent, result from human error. The safety equipment is okay and the safety rules seem okay. The average age of employees in this plant is comparable to that of employees in plants with better safety records, so age does not seem to be a factor.

Wage earners say that the bad accident record is caused by "them." The "them" identified is top management. When asked for evidence, the wage earners say such things as "We used to have fifteen safety inspectors who constantly reviewed our working practices. But to save a nickel 'they' decided to make safety a line responsibility. Now we have only two people assigned to safety. Without safety inspectors, the line doesn't know how to spot safety problems any better than we do."

Another comment is, "Whenever a special project had an element of risk to it, we always paired up to do the job. 'They' decided it was less efficient for two to be assigned when one could do the job. Now whenever comparable projects arise, we have to do them alone, and if a person gets in trouble there is no one to help him out."

The foremen feel that the "them-ism" is partly valid, too, but in a different way. Foremen say, "The pressure for production is so great that we have to cut corners. Sometimes safety is sacrificed. If we weren't pushed so hard we could work at a more leisurely pace. This would reduce the readiness of people to take risks. They would have time to put the last turn on the bolt rather than leave it loose in order to get to the next one."

Top management says, "There is no more production pressure in this plant than in any other. The equipment is good, the safety rules are sound, and the studies show that the accidents are avoidable for the most part. The problem is in the workforce. When it is not personally concerned about safety, accidents happen."

The people at the top authorize a special safety school to reinforce the safety rules in the minds of those most at risk, explaining the proper use of safety equipment and so on. This is coupled with a crash communications program to rivet everyone's attention on the importance of safety. Yet the problem remains.

The vice-president calls you in to discuss this situation. He wants your perception of the problem and your recommendation for coming to grips with it. Is this an attitude problem or not? What do you recommend as the basis for bringing about a change in attitudes to support safe working practices?

Example 3   Union–Management Relations

A company has had bad relations with the union over the years. It is now confronted with a worsening relationship after a recent strike that embittered everyone and brought production to a halt. Corporate leadership is finally realizing that either the union must be "replaced" or a problem-solving relationship must be created that will permit productivity to increase and allow the company to make good on its promises to customers.

Management consists of 300 people who have negative feelings toward and are deeply frustrated by the union. It is generally acknowledged within management that the union is "up to no good" and that its sole interest is in digging more and more out of management while bargaining for more restrictive practices that have a negative influence on productivity. Yet on several occasions the union has been extremely cooperative when the company faced a different kind of financial catastrophe. Is this an attitude problem or not? What are your recommendations to senior management for changing the union–management relationship?

Attitudes Toward Productivity

These three situations are by no means uncommon. In many respects they reflect the kinds of problems we have all come to accept and live with. As a result they are sometimes so taken for granted that it is difficult even to see them as problems. Yet each reflects a basic attitude toward the work situation. The more realistic prospect for alleviating them is to bring about changes in the attitudes that caused them.

We need to understand how attitudes toward productivity that are shared by several people come into existence, how they are shaped, and under what circumstances they come to be maintained over long periods of time, sometimes without any significant change. We also need to learn under what circumstances it is possible for an entire group to reexamine its attitudes and change them. Finally, we need to explore how an organization can go about strengthening its performance through bringing attitudes that support productivity into existence.

A key link in accounting for higher or lower productivity

is the *attitudes* toward productivity held by the people who work together. The important questions to be dealt with are: Is it possible for an organization deliberately and explicitly to manage the attitudes of those it employs? Can positive attitudes toward performance be brought about to achieve quality results and advance productivity while reducing waste, maintaining safety, and increasing creativity?

Many managers reject the notion that they are concerned with the management of attitudes. Various reasons are expressed, but they have an underlying theme. One manager says, "I'm managing results, not attitudes." Another says, "What I am managing is the behavior of people, not their attitudes. As long as people apply themselves to the work in the manner expected of them, that's all that counts."

Still another reaction is, "Attitudes don't exist, only behavior exists. You can't see attitudes, but you can see behavior. Treat people as though their heads were 'black boxes.' Don't try to read minds." Or, "Attitudes may be important, but you don't 'manage' them. You manage behavior. When behavior is consistent with the needs of the organization, people's attitudes will become consistent with their behavior." In other words, it is behavior that creates attitudes, not the other way around. All these remarks are consistent with the point of view of behaviorism, from Pavlov[1] to Watson[2] to Skinner.[3]

A different reaction points in the same direction. This view maintains that it is an invasion of privacy for a manager to deal with a subordinate in terms of attitudes. A person's attitudes are private business. A manager is being paid to promote the kind of *behavior* that contributes to productivity and nothing more should be expected.

These reactions reflect one side of a major controversy confronting modern management. The other side has a very different perspective. It asserts that attitudes toward productivity are all-important. Only when attitudes are managed well can productive results be anticipated. This point of view presumes that attitudes are antecedent to action.[4] Therefore, a negative attitude toward productivity can be expected to cause an individual to be less productive than if he or she embraced a positive attitude. Pressuring for productive behavior may merely cause the person to feel stress from being "coerced" and thus increase the negative attitude.

The point of view to be developed in this book is that through the sound management of attitudes toward productivity, it is possible to create an orientation that results in more productivity while retaining quality. To embrace this point of view is by no means to imply that those who see attitudes as personal or private and outside the scope of management are entirely wrong; there are categories of attitudes that have no relevance in the context of productivity. They include political persuasions, attitudes toward religion, and, in general, personal attitudes about family or private life. Yet it remains true that attitudes precede action, and if attitudes toward work are adverse to the wanted action, they will have a negative effect on the outcome.

NOTES

1. Pavlov's original research showed how a stimulus connects with a response. When the bell rang, the dog salivated because the bell had become connected to the likelihood of the dog's being fed. No attitudes were involved. See I. P. Pavlov, *Conditioned Reflexes*. New York: Oxford University Press, 1927.

2. One of the first applications of behaviorism to life problems was by J. B. Watson and R. Rayner, "Conditioned Emotional Reactions," *Journal of Experimental Psychology*, 1920, *3:* 1–14. Watson generalized and in many respects crystallized the field of behaviorism in his book *Behaviorism* (rev. ed.). Chicago: University of Chicago Press, 1962.

3. Skinner has not only contributed to basic research, but has also been one of the most successful popularizers of the field of behaviorism. His most important work is B. F. Skinner, *The Behavior of Organisms*. New York: Appleton-Century-Crofts, 1938. His most controversial book, one that has given

more impetus to an examination of behaviorism from the standpoint of its practical ramifications, is *Beyond Freedom and Dignity*. New York: Vintage Books, 1971.

4. One of the original formulations of the central role of attitudes as antecedent to behavior is by W. I. Thomas and F. Znaniecki, *The Polish Peasant in Europe and America*. Chicago: University of Chicago Press, 1918.

Sherif's work on attitudes as frames of reference is also of importance. See M. Sherif, *The Psychology of Social Norms*. New York: Harper & Row, 1936. Stagner did some of the original important work on translating from theory to practice, particularly as attitudinal factors influencing union–management relations. See R. Stagner, *The Psychology of Industrial Conflict*. New York: Wiley, 1956.

Early applications of attitude research to the military are described in S. A. Stouffer, E. A. Suchmann, L. C. DeVinney, S. A. Star, and R. M. Williams, Jr., *The American Soldier*, Vol. 1, *Adjustments During Army Life*. Princeton, N.J.: Princeton University Press, 1949.

2
Group Norms and Personal Attitudes

We experience our attitudes toward productivity as private and personal, as originating in our own thinking, experience, and motivation, and as unique to each of us. What we fail to realize is that our attitudes arise from the norms of the organizational groups in which we hold memberships. As a result, group norms for productivity and our attitudes toward them regulate a greater part of our work effort or lack of it than we realize.

Defining Norms

A norm is any uniformity of attitude, opinion, feeling, or action shared by two or more people. Groups are characterized by the norms their members share. For all practical purposes, a group could not be a group if it lacked norms to regulate and coordinate interactions among members. The reason is that there would be no basis for coordination or cooperation. If norms were absent, we might refer to the individuals who are physically assembled in the same place as an *aggregate*, but not as a group.

17

The concept of norms and other concepts related to it (such as standards and traditions) are not often used to describe individuals. Groups have norms, but individuals usually are not pictured that way. We may speak of someone as having an attitude or attitudes, but it is more customary to speak of a group as having norms or traditions. Even though individuals are their "carriers," norms and traditions belong to groups, not individuals.

By contrast, concepts such as attitudes, opinions, and feelings convey something about individuals that groups may be said to lack. Individuals have opinions; groups do not. The same holds for attitudes and feelings. All these words describe something viewed from the perspective of the individual.[1]

How norms and attitudes are related can be seen in the following example. A family may arrange its activities so that everyone convenes for dinner at six. A norm has thus been established to which family members willingly adhere. It allows for an orderly and convenient gathering that gives the family an opportunity to discuss a variety of subjects and share their experiences. Our *attitudes* reflect this whenever we interrupt what we are doing in order to be home on time for dinner. The attitude is, "It's important to me to be home on time and not keep the others waiting." We don't say, "My family has a six o'clock norm," because we don't experience it that way. We say, "I want to get home by six so as to be with my family." That's an attitude toward the family, but supporting it is a family-based norm.

Another example is the get-together of family members at Christmas. It may not always be possible for every member to get home each year, but each member shares the norm. The correlated attitude expressed over the phone might be, "I'm so disappointed I can't be there, but I hope you have a wonderful holiday." Such a remark would make no sense if the norm of convening at Christmas did not prevail. Let someone not show and give no reason and those present would speculate on that person's motivation with a sense of disapproval. A norm prevails among family members, but it's not experienced that way. Each member feels he or she shares a personal attitude with those who think the same way.

Some of the obvious norms that exist at work are related to how people at various levels dress, when coffee breaks are taken and for how long, and, sometimes, whether managers leave the office with a briefcase.

These examples indicate how the term "norm" is being used: to describe regularities in behavior that characterize two or more members of a group. Even though we talk about our personal attitudes fairly freely as we go about our daily activities, we are responding to group-centered norms far more often than we realize. This comes into focus better if we look at the range of words that relate to the word "norm" when used in different contexts.

A "tradition," for example, is a norm established in the remote past that continues to influence our current behavior. A "precedent" is some action taken at a prior time that served to model a solution to a problem. It, too, has become a norm. A "habit" is a typical way of dealing with something almost automatically. Here again, the word "norm" appropriately describes what happens. A "rule" is an explicit statement of how something should be done. When people accept it as sound and okay, a rule takes on the status of a norm and also governs our attitudes toward the specified behavior. The same is true of a "regulation." It dictates how something is to be handled. It becomes a norm when those responsible for executing the regulation have come to accept it as appropriate. "Policy" also refers to desired uniformities of behavior that define strategic considerations of action. When behavior is consistent with policy, policy has become a norm. The term "standard operating procedure," or "SOP," also describes ways in which organization members are expected to act in carrying out their assigned job activities.

The same is true with regard to "rituals" and "rites." A ritual is a sequence of activities that unfold more or less in a fixed way, and since everyone knows the ritual, the norm for how to implement it is widely shared. A rite is the same.

Still other words that carry the notion of norms are "custom" and "taboo." A custom describes what group members are expected to do, while a taboo is a norm that describes what people are expected *not* to do. The phrase "informal system" has been used to characterize the unwritten rules—regulations, policies, traditions, precedents, standard operating procedures—that are not formalized in a documented sense but do govern how people act. The informal system is a normative one to which organization members are expected by other organization members to conform.

We can see from the above that many words in our language are used to convey the idea of a norm. A norm, then, is any uniformity of attitude or action that two or more people share by virtue of their membership in a group.

Norms and Behavior

Whenever two or more people share a group norm, it is likely they will also feel and express similar, if not identical, attitudes and values. These shared attitudes are difficult to see except when someone acts in a manner inconsistent with the norm. For example, if one member of a work group lets others carry the load, everyone else agrees that the member is a goldbrick and a negative attitude arises toward the shirker. By comparison, if one member of a work group goes all out and produces double everyone else's output, that individual is seen as an eager beaver. The group members have a negative attitude toward this person as well. We know this from experimental research.[2] People intuitively realize that, on the one hand, to fail to carry a share of the load is to suffer criticism; on the other hand, they also know that they court isolation or even ostracism if they push so hard that their behavior makes everyone else look inferior.

Norms regulate much of our lives—personal and family, career, and even recreation and leisure. These kinds of norms, therefore, regulate our productivity behavior.

Not all norms promote desirable behavior. A norm may be effective at an early stage and later become outmoded as a basis for interrelating with others in a situation where it is no longer applicable. When this occurs, the norm keeps us engaged in activities that have become irrelevant or even damaging. For example, a manager may state a norm—"It has been routine for us to change models on a five-year basis"—and explain it by saying "That's often enough," or "Innovations in technology can be collected and introduced economically once every few years rather than being brought in one at a time." The five-year model change period may be an outmoded tradition, as evidenced by other organizations that constantly change product lines to take advantage of innovative technology. Being more responsive to the consumer, they capture an increased share of the market. The key to whether a normative system is sound and valid is its ability to meet current requirements for product development and product modification.

The existence of a norm—and the attitudes that flow from it—is therefore highly significant. It can lead to promoting productivity or restricting output, to making decisions promptly or in a tortuously slow way, to exploiting opportunities or letting them pass almost unnoticed, to stifling or stimulating creativity, and so on. Because norms are so important, we need to understand much more about them. We need to know which conditions are favorable to their emergence, how they may be maintained at their best, how they can be restored if they have eroded, and how outmoded norms can be rejected and replaced by others that are supportive of sound behavior consistent with current requirements for productivity.

NOTES

1. The relationship between personal attitudes, group norms, and behavior is described in detail by D. R. Heise, "Group Dynamics and Attitude–Behavior Patterns." *Sociological Methods and Research*, 1977, *5*(3): 259–288.

2. An early and dramatic demonstration of how norms reduce productivity is reported by D. Roy, "Quota Restrictions and Goldbricking in a Machine Shop," *American Journal of Sociology*, 1952, *57*(5): 427–432. How a group makes a scapegoat of any member who breaks the norm and exceeds others in productivity has been demonstrated in L. Coch and J. R. P. French, "Overcoming Resistance to Change," *Human Relations*, 1948, *1*(4): 512–532.

3
How Norms Arise

It is important to realize that norms and attitudes are closely related. Both refer to the same phenomena looked at from two different perspectives. In one case the view is from the perspective of the group, and in the other it is from the perspective of the individual.

What this means in practical, everyday terms is that individuals pick up their attitudes, opinions, feelings, and actions from the groups to which they belong. Yet when we examine our own personal attitudes, opinions, and feelings, we tend to think of them as private and unique. Because these attitudes, opinions, and feelings seem natural and internally consistent, they appear to us to originate in our private thinking and to have little relationship to our group memberships.

Thus we are faced with a dilemma. Research leads us in the direction of seeing that our attitudes are shaped by our group memberships, and our subjective experiences confirm to us that our attitudes come from personal thinking and judgment. How is the contradiction resolved?

Even though they are the same in real life, for analytical purposes we need to separate the two phenomena: we must

23

view the formation of norms from the group perspective and the formation of attitudes, opinions, feelings, and actions from the individual perspective.

One of the difficulties in understanding how people come to share attitudes, opinions, feelings, and actions is that we rarely can observe them in the context of their origin and track the changes that occur in them as people who share them engage in give-and-take. We know, for example, that in any situation where several people work closely together productivity is a norm that has arisen over the years and has become stable and consistent for that group. We know this from the individual perspective as well, because when any member of the group slacks off others express their negative attitudes toward this behavior by barbs and by making the slacker the butt of their jokes. The same thing happens with the person who violates the norms by pushing production too hard. Other people point a finger in such an antagonistic way as to bring that person's productivity back to the norm.

How the productivity norm is established and how it becomes stabilized as time passes is so complex a process that it defies everyday observation. Under these conditions we need to turn to research in social psychology. The research we want to study involves people coming together for the first time and sharing a novel experience. It is important that the experience be novel—that none of the participants has prior knowledge of the situation. Furthermore, the entire setting needs to be arranged so that what happens between the individuals can be measured over time and according to systematic analysis.

At first glance you may doubt that these experiments have any relevance to understanding productivity on the shop floor. As will become clear, however, such doubts are unjustified, because only by understanding the principles involved do we have any chance of increasing productivity through the better management and supervision of work group norms.

Convergence and the Formation of Norms

One of the first empirical demonstrations of how norms take shape was carried out by Sherif.[1] It involved a special kind of novel experience based on the phenomenon known as the *autokinetic effect*. The autokinetic effect occurs when a person looks at a pinpoint of light in a totally darkened room and experiences the light as moving. The movement seems to have an objective reality, even though the point of light is actually fixed. The reason for the apparent motion of the stationary light is that when a room is pitch black there is no visual framework for "anchoring" the light. The situation is identical with the experience of lying on the ground in the dark and seeing a star move through the heavens. The star does not move as the eye experiences it, but the observer feels keenly that the star did in fact move. In both cases, what is observed is *apparent* movement rather than real movement.

In the absence of a visual framework for anchoring the pinpoint of light in a stable way, the amount of movement that is apparent to different individuals will vary widely. One person may describe it as moving a few inches, whereas another may see it as moving a few feet.

In one experiment, based on Sherif's work, several people who have never experienced the autokinetic phenomenon are brought together and assembled in a darkened room. We turn the pinpoint of light on for a brief period. Then we ask each person to report, in the presence of others, the amount of movement observed. We do this a number of times, each time turning the light off between trials.

What we notice after the first few trials is that the amounts of movement experienced by different individuals tend to come closer and closer together. Let's say that in the initial report on Trial 1 person *A* indicated that the light moved 2 feet, person *B* said it moved 1 foot, and person *C* indicated it moved 3 inches. On Trial 2 person *A*'s report of movement drops to 18 inches. Person *B*'s report stays at 1 foot. Person *C* now reports movement to have been 6 or 8 inches. In the space of a few more trials each person can be expected to report that the light is moving about a foot. A high degree of consistency between the different viewers becomes evident.

This experiment demonstrates the phenomenon of *convergence.* This occurs whenever there is little or no prior basis for reacting to an experience and others are experiencing the same phenomenon and expressing their reactions to it. Although personal reactions vary widely at first, as experience increases reactions tend to come together—that is, to converge. Now in much the same way people come to share a similar perspective. Social reality has been created through the process of convergence, and this coming together around a single set of attitudes, opinions, feelings, or actions constitutes a norm.[2]

Aftereffects of Convergence

Just because convergence has occurred, it is by no means the end of the process. There are aftereffects in the sense that attitudes, opinions, feelings, and actions tend to persist on an individual-by-individual basis long after group members have stopped meeting. This is demonstrated in the following way.

After the experiment ends, we ask a neutral experimenter, a person unknown to the participants, to interview them one at a time and to get their reactions to the experience. We expect the participant to say something like this: "I became more expert in my opinions with each new trial, until I felt quite objective about my reports." Then the interviewer might ask, "Were you ever influenced by the reports of others?" The participant is likely to answer, "No, I don't think so." Or, "Possibly a little, but it was not important." Alternatively, the participant might say, "Maybe, but in the opposite direction, because I thought they were wrong."

These interviews permit us to infer that participants' attitudes, opinions, feelings, and actions were far more influenced by other people than they recognized. This is important, because precisely the same things are happening on the shop floor.

The existence of aftereffects can be demonstrated in another way. Participants who are not interviewed on their experience might be called back to the laboratory and asked to make a second round of estimates. This time they judge the amount of movement by themselves rather than in the presence of others. Now their reports tend to be about a foot, which was what the group judgments had hovered around during the initial experience. Although some of these participants report less and others more movement than they had come to "see" during the initial experiment when reporting in the presence of others, their reports are closer to the "norm" than the reports they made prior to the phenomenon of convergence. This demonstrates that once convergence occurs it has a persistent influence on how people react to future experiences of the same kind. It has also been observed that people deny with increasing conviction that others have had any influence on them. By now judgments are experienced as strictly personal. The influence of norms on personal attitudes is by this time firm, but people completely miss it.

The contradiction introduced at the beginning of this chapter can now be understood: others have an impact on us through the process of convergence. However, because each of us is an individual, and because for the most part we have not become expert in identifying or calibrating the effect other people have on us, we tend to exaggerate the degree of independence that we are able to maintain.[3] We each tend to think that we work at our own pace, but to a significant degree the actual pace is called by the group as drummer.

Simple though it is, this experiment (and many others of similar character) clarifies a significant factor in social life. This factor is convergence. Convergence explains how people tend to shift their attitudes, opinions, feelings, and actions toward one another. When we realize that much of industrial life fits this mold—by virtue of people expressing attitudes, opinions, and feelings that result in people coming to think and act in much the same way—we also realize that convergence can operate strongly to influence personal behavior. The experimental also demonstrates that even though convergence is influencing individuals, people don't necessarily experience themselves as having accepted influence. Rather, they feel that their attitudes, opinions, feelings, and actions retain a personal character that is unique and that "belongs" to them alone.

Convergence in Organizational Life

Two young people at the beginning of their careers join a company, one as a management trainee and the other as a manual worker. Neither knows very much about business. When it comes to having an attitude toward profit and profitability, they are at about the same point. Neither has much of an opinion one way or the other.

As the person who joins management acquires experience, he or she comes to develop a positive attitude toward profit and profitability and can give sound reasons for that attitude. "You need profitability to keep an organization moving and to provide the products and services that society has to have in this day and age. Without profit there would be no incentive." If you ask this person where the attitude came from, the response would probably be, "Well, I more or less thought this thing out by myself. I've just expressed a self-evident truth." If you ask whether the job as a member of management had anything to do with the person's attitude, the reply is likely to be, "Well, many people think as I do, but it's not that we've influenced one another. Rather, it's that each of us, confronted with the same basic issue, has reasoned it out in our own way. That we seem to have comparable attitudes by no means implies that we have been influenced by one another."

Based on the research presented up to this point, we would surmise that the management trainee has been influenced by his or her managerial colleagues, and that the opinion expressed resulted from the trainee's convergence to the management group norm relating to profitability.

Now let's track the employee who came in as a manual worker. In time, the employee joins the union and becomes an officer in it. If we probe his or her attitudes and opinions on the same question, the union officer might say, "Profit and profitability are okay for the bosses, but they come from exploitation of the worker and result in millionaires who contribute little while living off the fat of the land. It may be our system, but it sure leaves a lot to be desired." If we were to ask this person where he or she got these ideas, the reply might be, "I looked around and examined the evidence. It led me to my own conclusions." If we then asked if he or she were influenced by fellow workers or other union officers, the response might be, "No, I don't think so. We're a pretty independent bunch. Several people look at the same data and arrive at the same conclusions, but that doesn't mean they influence one another."

These two examples provide a good illustration of the phenomenon of convergence. In each case, the final attitude around which convergence occurs depends on the norms of the group within which the person holds membership.

Let us add an additional twist. In the course of time the person who entered the company as a manual worker is offered an opportunity to become a manager, possibly because of demonstrated leadership ability as a union officer. He or she accepts. A few months later the new manager is again queried on attitudes and opinions toward profit and profitability. Answers are quite different now. In fact, they are almost identical to those of the person who originally entered industry on the management side. Having shifted membership, this person has also shifted thinking, influenced by the new affiliation. Attitudes converge until they approximate the norms of the new membership group. It is a good bet that the employee would not be completely aware that his or her attitude toward profit and profitability had undergone a 180-degree turn.

Examples such as these suggest why people develop the attitudes, opinions, and feelings they do. They also tell us something about the ways in which a person's attitudes may be subject to change under "natural" conditions.

Though convergence is a basic social process, we know far less about it than we need in order to understand how norms emerge in everyday life. One of the reasons is that convergence happens quickly, when attention is focused elsewhere. Moreover, once convergence has occurred, it feels so natural that people fail to recognize its existence. Therefore the influence it exerts is almost invisible.

Physical Versus Social Reality

Convergence often occurs in a spontaneous and what appears to be a natural way. There is no reason *why* convergence should exist and result in the formation of norms—the fact is that it does. We need to understand the conditions that promote convergence and the emergence of norms.

There are two kinds of reality: physical (or empirical) reality, which is objective in nature, and social (or experiential) reality, which is subjective in nature. Norms arise more readily when circumstances are subject to interpretation than when circumstances have an objective character that can be proved.[4]

Let us begin with physical reality. There is, out there, an empirical reality that the evidence of our senses confirms. We turn on a switch and a light appears; we turn it off and the light disappears. We infer a physical reality. Something is out there. We see an automobile coming toward us head on. It crashes into our fender. We know that two objects were trying to occupy the same space simultaneously, and the empirical reality is that they could not. We are so familiar with physical reality that we need not try to verify its independent existence. We know it exists. In the absence of evidence from others that contradicts our senses, our experience of it is usually adequate for dealing with it. In this category, norms have little bearing on our behavior.

Experiential, or social, reality comes about when we confront a situation in which our knowledge of physical reality is not pertinent. We look into the sky in the pitch of night and see a point of light moving. Is it a meteor? Could it be some man-made vehicle in outer space? We simply do not know. We have no knowledge of the physical world that will tell us. Under these conditions we turn to other people—first to check out whether they experienced the same phenomenon and next to gain their version of it in order to test what the experience may imply. What they report has been demonstrated to have a profound effect on how we see things. It is under those conditions—when "reality" is subject to a variety of interpretations—that norms most readily emerge, norms that thereafter control our conduct. The experiment dealing with the apparent movement of a fixed point of light is comparable. It is an example of a reality defined by the norms of social judgment.

A great part of daily life is governed by social reality, premised on norms regarding what is right, what is wrong, what is good, what is bad, what is okay, and what is not okay. We know, for example, that thoughtless criticism of another person can be painful, so we develop and share with many others an anti-candor norm. That is, we come to an agreement, usually a silent one, as to what we can say and what probably would be better left unspoken. Much of social reality is of this nature. It results from our membership in various groups. As adults, we find that some experiential reality comes to have an absolute quality in its own right, even though its origins and continued maintenance are based on attitudes arising from norms that are widely shared. We think it is unique and personal to each of us, but in fact it is not. If others challenge it, we stick by our guns and resist being influenced by them.

The norms that arise from the comparisons we make with other people in our social framework form the basis for the way we interpret social reality. Since we have no physical knowledge or experience to guide us, we turn to others and use them as data points and, in a certain sense, as judges who are independent of us. As a result, we allow others to exert the greatest influence on us in circumstances where reality is subject to interpretation. More often than not, we do not recognize this influence. Because we fail to pay attention to it, we do not see or hear it.

This is all highly pertinent to issues of productivity, and yet these subtle and perverse influences do not stand out in the everyday routines in which we are involved. It is somewhat easier to see them in situations that are outside our routines. For example, the phenomenon of convergence is apparent when a new technology is introduced and people who must implement it are unfamiliar with the new machinery involved—how to operate it, at what speed, and so on. As group members interact, convergence takes place and a rate or level of productivity becomes established for that group. The same process of convergence occurs in starting up a new plant, opening a new office, or deciding how to penetrate a new market.

The operation of convergence also becomes somewhat more visible when a group of managers is confronted with an unconventional problem. Manager *A* thinks the solution ought to be approached one way, manager *B* another, and manager *C* a third. As they discuss their perceptions of the problem, they quickly converge on a single approach. After that a solution can be pursued in a cooperative way.

Another example: A certification election occurs and a union gains the right to organize the work force and represent it in its relations with management. Members of management have widely diverse views on how best to deal with the union. As these are voiced, discussed, and deliberated, an approach begins to take shape, again revealing the role of convergence in managerial decision making.

What we see in each of these examples is that convergence toward a common position is an almost invisible process. It is second nature to all those involved.

NOTES

1. Standard research utilizing the autokinetic phenomenon was carried out by M. Sherif, "A Study of Some Social Factors in Perception." *Archives of Psychology*, 1935, *187*. An additional description of this research that gives introspective reports by experimental subjects is M. Sherif, "An Experimental Approach to the Study of Attitudes," *Sociometry*, 1937, *1*(1 and 2): 90–98.

2. The original scientific observation of the convergence phenomenon is described in F. H. Allport, *Social Psychology*. Boston: Houghton Mifflin, 1924.

3. This conclusion is corroborated in S. E. Asch, "Studies of Independence and Conformity: A Minority of One Against a Unanimous Majority," *Psychological Monographs*, 1956, *70*(9), Whole No. 416.

4. The distinction between physical and social reality was used importantly by Festinger in his theory of cognitive dissonance and has been retained as an important distinction in pertinent research since that time. See L. Festinger, *A Theory of Cognitive Dissonance*. Stanford: Stanford University Press, 1957; L. Festinger, *Conflict, Decision and Dissonance*. Stanford University Press, 1964.

4
The Formation of Groups

What causes one person to join one group and another to join a different group? This is an important question for management selection, promotion, and advancement. It is also basic to understanding the formation of norms and the dynamics of conformity.

Two quite different explanations are possible. One is that we seek out others who are different from us, people who are unique and distinctive. They are stimulating to us. The proposition is that opposites attract. Sameness is dull, difference challenging. This is a very likely proposition and, indeed, many people feel that it is basically a true explanation.

The other explanation is that we seek out others who are like us. According to this view, we feel secure when we find that others share our points of view, and we feel threatened when others' attitudes, opinions, and feelings are different from our own.

If the first proposition is true, our attitudes, opinions, and feelings are likely to be in a constant state of flux. We continuously hear different points of view that cause us to reexamine and modify those we hold.

If the other point of view is valid—birds of a feather—our attitudes, opinions, feelings, and actions are likely to become stabilized over time. We continuously hear ideas and opinions that reinforce our own.

The "opposites attract" view *is* valid, for a small number of situations. But research gives overwhelming support to the second proposition.

People tend to like others whose ideas, attitudes, and opinions are similar to theirs and to dislike those whose attitudes, opinions, feelings, and actions are significantly different. The result is that in everyday life a person comes to spend more time with those who think the same way and to spend less time with people who are significantly different. Voluntary groups, then, form around people who share the same or approximately the same attitudes, opinions, feelings, and actions.[1]

Cohesion and the Formation of Groups

Though personal preferences carry very little weight when management groups are put together—competence to do a job is central—the same dynamics apply: people prefer to associate with people they like and by whom they are liked. This is the phenomenon of *cohesion*.

One way of becoming more familiar with this phenomenon is to study it where it can most readily be seen—in situations where people who have had little or no prior contact are brought together. One such situation is a cocktail party. Almost as soon as people begin to congregate they seem to segregate, with the men coming together conversationally and the women doing the same. This is explained by the fact that the men have something in common, usually related to business and work, and therefore find it more comfortable to talk with one another than to cross the sex barrier and converse with women, whose life experiences are often quite different. On the other hand, women seem to find it more comfortable to share their experiences with one another. These experiences may also involve work, but issues centering on family, children, and homemaking provide stronger commonality.

Such segregation reveals the operation of cohesion: people who share certain attitudes or experiences seek out and associate with one another.

A dramatic example is provided by Malcolm X, an American black who became a Muslim and who was one of the first, if not *the* first, American ever to have participated in hajj. Hajj is the annual pilgrimage to Mecca that is part of the Muslim religious celebration.

Malcolm X, who supported an independent nationhood for black Americans rather than integration as the solution to the race problem, was very sensitive to social interactions. After his own pilgrimage to Mecca, he made the following comments about the cohesion he observed:

> There was a color pattern in the huge crowds. Once I happened to notice this, I closely observed it thereafter. Being from America made me intensely sensitive to matters of color. I saw that people who looked alike drew together and most of the time stayed together. This was entirely voluntary; there being no other reason for it, but Africans were with Africans, Pakistanis were with Pakistanis, and so on. I tucked it into my mind that when I returned home I would tell Americans of this observation: that where true brotherhood existed among all colors, where no one felt segregated, where there was no "superiority" complex, no "inferiority" complex—then voluntarily, naturally, people of the same kind felt drawn together by that which they had in common.[2]

There are many social bases for birds of a feather flocking together. People of like educational background tend to associate. Thus college graduates are more likely to collaborate with one another than with people who have only completed grade school. The latter, in turn, feel more comfortable interacting with others of like educational achievement. Indeed, this is the basis for what has become widely known in industry as the technical-practical distinction. Technical people know, understand, and interact with one another; practical people do the same, but technical and practical people have trouble interacting.

Socioeconomic level is another important basis for people drawing together. Those with similar wealth tend to congregate and sometimes to establish enclaves, communities into which people of lesser or newer wealth are not invited.

People who share the same religion also form associations, interacting with one another above and beyond the functional reason of worshiping together. They share attitudes that enable them to understand one another better and therefore to feel comfortable in less formal or more intimate circumstances.

Congregating around common interests, common values, or common attitudes constitutes one of the most significant bases of social organization. Within such groups, norms arise quickly because each member allows himself or herself to be influenced by the opinions, attitudes, and feelings of others he or she likes. Cohesion, in other words, accelerates convergence toward, and adoption of, shared norms. A number of studies[3] demonstrate that regardless of the source of attraction to the group, the same dynamic seems to apply: the more attractive the group is to the individual, the greater the influence the group is able to exert on that person.

Cohesion in Organizational Life

Recognizing that we like those with whom we agree aids us in understanding what happens in organizational life. From the standpoint of promotion and advancement, bosses like subordinates who share their outlook. Thus, when a subordinate embraces norms held by the boss, this sharing may become an influential factor in the boss's decision to advance that subordinate. By the same token, the subordinate's feelings of cohesion with the boss may be reinforced, because the subordinate may allow himself or herself to be influenced by the boss by virtue of positive feelings about that boss.

Just as people develop feelings about one another, so people develop feelings about the organization for which they work. One attitude is, "This is the best company in the world. I want to spend all my working life here." Another: "This place is a dump. The quicker I can escape and get a decent job, the better."

Given these feelings of attraction and disenchantment, it follows that the person who experiences positive feelings toward the organization accepts the norms and values of the organization and is influenced by them, and the person who is disenchanted—that is, who has negative feelings—resists the organization. Several studies[4] shed light on these patterns.

In one study by Dittes and Kelley, group members were given ratings of the degree to which others present liked them and wished them to remain in the discussion. Those who had very low acceptance, who had the lowest index of private conformity, showed the highest degree of public conformity. Those who had received average acceptance exhibited the greatest shift toward the group view, indicating a consistency in private conviction and public expression. The finding implies that people whose acceptance is weak or average are probably least secure and most susceptible to pressure.

In another experiment, Jackson and Saltzstein varied both the level of congeniality—that is, how attractive the individual found the group to be—and the level of acceptance and/or rejection. The four conditions were (1) psychological membership, in which the person had high acceptance by the group and high attraction to it; (2) psychological non-membership, in which the person had low acceptance by the group and low attraction to it; (3) preference group membership, in which the person had low acceptance by the group but high attraction to it; and (4) marginal group membership, in which the person had high acceptance by the group but low attraction to it.

Members worked in groups of four or five under two different orientations: a *normative* condition, in which group competed against group; and a *modal* condition, under which members were compared as individuals. Conformity was greater in the group than in the individual situation and greater in the high-attraction than in the low-attraction situation. However, conformity under the low-attraction condition was uniformly higher than had been predicted. Telling subjects, first, that their performance was inferior and, second, that they were least accepted apparently led to feelings of rejection *and* anxiety and to higher conformity.

Thibaut and Strickland conducted studies in which they varied pressure by having people express high, moderate, or low confidence in members working under either a task orientation (solving problems) or a cohesiveness orientation (maintaining group membership). For subjects given the task orientation, conformity decreased as pressures increased. For those given the group membership orientation, conformity increased as other members, by ballot, showed increased confidence in their judgments. The study demonstrates the greater susceptibility to conformity of individuals motivated to maintain group membership.

Convergence, Cohesion, and Productivity

These two factors—convergence toward norms following others as data points and cohesion among those who like one another and hold common attitudes—are important for understanding productivity. If group members like one another and the productivity norm is high, it is likely that positive attitudes toward productivity will be shared and consistent among the group members. Members will then say, "It's important to put in a good day's work. You feel satisfied with yourself." It is unlikely that anyone's opinion will be very different from that voiced by anyone else. Certainly any member who departs very far from the productivity norm will be in trouble even though each member is likely to think that his or her opinions, attitudes, and feelings are arrived at independently. Furthermore, the more cohesive the group, the greater the acceptance and support of the norm.

The pervasiveness of these influences is much more evident when examined from a group rather than an individualistic perspective. For example, return on investment (ROI) or other indicators of organizational performance may come to have the property of a norm. When a low level of ROI is a shared norm in a cohesive group, decision making comes to be consistent with producing this level of ROI. By comparison, when a high level of ROI is set by a cohesive top group and constitutes a shared norm, decision making comes to be consistent with producing ROI at this level. Therefore, two companies in the same business, operating in the same markets, may differ markedly in earnings capacity because of the profitability norms that prevail in each.

We see, then, that norms—standards and traditions—are a sound basis for understanding how groups behave and for understanding how people's attitudes, opinions, and feelings are formed and maintained.[5] Norms come into being because of two considerations: the convergence that results from comparisons where social reality is the issue and the convergence that results from people's liking one another. Because social reality contains no absolutes, as does the world of physical reality, there's no fixed answer to how much production can be judged poor, acceptable, or excellent. It follows that a norm regarding how much production is enough comes into existence as a result of these convergence phenomena.

NOTES

1. A series of studies by Byrne over 15 years demonstrates the strong relationship between similarity of attitudes, feelings, behavior, and attraction. The different kinds of similarity studied included economic grounds (D. Byrne, G. J. Clore, Jr., and P. Worchel, "Effective Economic Similarity/Dissimilarity on Interpersonal Attraction," *Journal of Personality and Social Psychology*, 1966, *4:* 220–224); personality characteristics (D. Byrne, W. Griffitt, and D. Stefaniak, "Attraction and Similarity of Personality Characteristics," *Journal of Personality and Social Psychology*, 1967, *5:* 82–29); and similarity of attitudes (D. Byrne and D. Nelson, "Attraction as a Linear Function of Proportion of Positive Reinforcement," *Journal of Personality and Social Psychology*, 1965, *1:* 659–663). These studies demonstrate that the more similar people are in their attitudes, the more attracted to each other they will be.

2. From *The Autobiography of Malcolm X*. New York: Grove Press, 1964, p. 349. Experimental studies of housing projects demonstrate that this same factor as applied to race also applies to people who are friends with one another. When a housing unit is mixed racially and in age groups, friendship is based on similarity of age and race, with 60 percent of reported friends being in the same age category and approximately 70 percent being of the same race. See L. Nahemow and N. M. P. Lawton, "Similarity and Propinquity in Friendship Formation," *Journal of Personality and Social Psychology*, 1975, *32:* 205–213.

3. See H. B. Gerard, "The Anchorage of Opinions in Face-to-Face Groups," *Human Relations*, 1954, *7:* 313–325. Attraction has also been studied in terms of the personal attractiveness of the partner and the prestige of the group in the eyes of its members. See K. Back, "Influence Through Social Communication," *Journal of Abnormal and Social Psychology*, 1951, *46:* 9–23.

It can be inferred from a study by Sakura that even where the activity of the group is abstract or where measures of success are delayed for many years, cohesion is a major factor in promoting conformity. See M. M. Sakura, "Small-Group Cohesiveness and Detrimental Conformity," *Sociometry*, 1975, *38*(2): 340–357.

4. J. E. Dittes and H. H. Kelley, "Effect of Different Conditions of Acceptance upon Conformity to Group Norms," *Journal of Abnormal and Social Psychology*, 1938, *33:* 489–507. J. M. Jackson and H. D. Saltzstein, "The Effect of Person–Group Relationships on Conformity Processes," *Journal of Abnormal and Social Psychology*, 1958, *57:* 17–24. J. W. Thibaut and L. Strickland, "Psychological Set and Social Conformity," *Journal of Personality*, 1956, *25:* 115–129.

5. The distribution of attitudes around norms has been pictured as taking three different forms: a Gaussian curve, a U-shaped curve, and a J-shaped curve.

Within the framework of corporate life, the Gaussian distribution is a better basis for picturing the range of diverse attitudes around a central trend, while the U-shaped distribution is a better basis for understanding attitudes in loosely organized systems such as is characterized by the polarization of attitudes in political parties in the United States. The J-shaped curve may be the best distribution for conformity to norms that have only a one-sided distribution. See G. Paicheler, "Norms and Attitude Change 1: Polarization and Styles of Behavior," *European Journal of Social Psychology*, 1976, *6*(4): 405–427; and F. H. Allport, "The J-Curve Hypothesis of Conforming Behavior," *Journal of Social Psychology*, 1934, *5:* 141–183.

5
The Pressure to Conform

Once convergence has taken place, thoughts, feelings, attitudes, and actions among members become more uniform. Now the norm becomes a standard. Every member is presumed to accept the norm as a basis for attitude, opinion, and action, regardless of whether he or she privately agrees with it. Conformity is the word for behaving and expressing opinions consistent with group norms—that is, for complying with group attitudes and expectations. Sometimes a person expresses compliance outwardly, while maintaining inner reservations, but for the moment we are concerned with the *appearance* of compliance.

How Conformity Works

The following example demonstrates the operation of conformity. A corporation is not unionized. The desire to maintain its nonunion status expresses the prevailing attitude throughout management. The norm is revealed in such statements as "The company has far more flexibility this way," and "We manage better when we don't have a union between ourselves and the employee."

Now a member of management expresses a different opinion, speaking in favor of a union for employees and offering arguments in support of this position. The manager says, "Unions have brought the American worker greater material benefits and security than workers anywhere else in the free world. A union makes life simpler because it provides a mechanism for the expression and resolution of grievances. Management speaks with a single voice. Why not employees?"

A member of management has taken a deviant point of view and advocated a union arrangement in this nonunion company. Two consequences can be predicted. The first is that colleagues will apply pressure to get this person back into line. Everyone concentrates on persuading this person to "quit kidding around" or to come back into the fold under the premise that "you've lost your senses." The pressure is likely to be uniform and intense. Probably no one takes the time to seriously review the merits and demerits of the pro-union argument.

After a period of time, if the deviant persists and demonstrates that he or she is not going to return to the fold, a second reaction sets in. Now colleagues turn away. They ignore the deviant and isolate him or her. This isolation spreads to issues far beyond the single matter of pro-union advocacy. Soon the deviant finds that others do not consult as they once had, that he or she is not invited to attend all meetings, and so on. Sometimes in the aftermath of such pulling away from a shared norm, the deviant finds that promotions are delayed, and employment may even be terminated. The termination, of course, is not for a pro-union attitude but for some other reason—such as "Too difficult to get along with" or "The chemistry was wrong."

These social forces are powerful enough to keep us all in line. Unfortunately, in terms of creativity, "in line" all too often means adhering to norms and clinging to attitudes that may be out of touch with the needs of the organization and even out of kilter with the times. As a result, important innovations are not made, and there is a heavy price to pay.

The automobile industry offers a striking example of adherence to outmoded norms. Throughout the 1970s foreign carmakers increased their share of the American market by introducing small, energy-efficient automobiles. The American automobile industry seemed unable to read the signs of the times and continued to produce large automobiles that were energy-inefficient and more costly than foreign cars.

The first energy crisis of 1973 should have been enough to jolt the American car industry out of its prevailing "big car" norm, but it did little to shift either that norm or the basic attitudes maintained within the automobile industry. Only with the constantly advancing costs of energy and the deeper market penetration by foreign car manufacturers have the large American carmakers begun to shift, seeing that the future inevitably will compel them in the direction of energy-efficient automobile manufacturing.

Pressuring managers to accept the status quo in these circumstances is described as one of the deterrents to change in the General Motors Corporation, as revealed in this remark to a member who pleaded for innovation: "You're not being a team player."[1]

The Dynamics of Conformity

These are the kinds of conformity pressures that operate to keep the status quo intact, even when the norm has become outmoded. What do we know of these processes from behavioral science research? Let us use a basic behavioral science experiment[2] to illuminate the underlying dynamics of conformity pressure. Seven people in a group read the case of Johnny Rocco, a young boy who has acted badly. The case is concerned with the best method for handling Johnny as he enters senior high school. The issue is whether Johnny should be given love or punishment, and to what degree. The case is written in such a way that most people agree that love is more likely to bring Johnny around than punishment.

Since there is no physical reality, we see in this experiment how pressures to conform are applied when the bases for exercising judgment are social and experiential reality. As the seven people begin to discuss the issue, they soon find themselves in approximate agreement. The agreement begins to emerge as a norm of shared commitment. Now a late member joins the group and advocates punishment—not the severest possible, but strong enough to get Johnny to recognize the inappropriateness of his ways. Attention shifts in a dramatic way. This person must be persuaded that punishment is inappropriate. The other members communicate with the deviant, expressing a variety of arguments to persuade him or her to come around to their point of view. Few try to probe this position or to understand its rationale, and there is no serious effort to examine a solution different from the one they have already agreed on.

Once arguments against the punishment approach have been exhausted and the punishment advocate continues to maintain an independent position, the seven somehow turn away from the deviant, who continues to maintain his or her distinctive position. The seven agree among themselves on the love treatment and act as though the punishment advocate no longer existed. The deviant is effectively isolated; the group goes on about its business and ceases directing communication toward this person. Thus we see that when efforts to persuade the deviant to change position are unsuccessful, he or she is ignored.

This experiment examined another question: How much do participants like or come to dislike the deviant? The issue of acceptance versus rejection is basic to cohesion. Those who participate in the experiment do not know that the advocate of punishment has been instructed to adopt that position as part of the experiment. This fact is revealed only after the following step has been completed.

Group members are told that the group will be meeting again but will have to reduce its size. The members are asked to rank all other people in the group for preference of inclusion in another discussion, unrelated to the Johnny Rocco case. The nominations are studied for the frequency with which each of the group members is eliminated from future membership. It is another way of examining cohesion. The question is whether the group members will accept the advocate of punishment as often as they accept the advocates of love. If they do, then the factor of cohesion— that like-minded people enjoy one another—is disproved.

The empirical result is that the punishment advocate is left out of membership in a future group significantly more often than representatives of the love approach. In fact, people do prefer others who agree with them. The deviant, though ignored after he or she fails to be persuaded, is by no means forgotten; he or she is actively rejected from membership in future groups.

This experiment reveals a basic aspect of group dynamics that operates to enforce conformity: the price of continued deviation from a group norm is rejection.[3]

Now we have a behavioral science basis for understanding the fate of the manager who took a pro-union position in a nonunionized company, or the General Motors executive who challenged the big car norm. For a certain period of time the manager was the target of efforts by others to swing him or her to their point of view. With continued resistance, the manager was ignored but not forgotten and later received adverse treatment and eventual dismissal.

Innumerable instances of this phenomenon exist throughout business and industry. It can be seen in applied research laboratories where a Ph.D. chemist resists buckling down and doing applied work, maintaining a degree of "purity" in research designs that others feel is unnecessary. Refusing to take shortcuts, the chemist eventually is walled off and, if at all antagonistic, is likely to be seen as a bull in the china shop. Eventually, the purist departs, finding the place "impossible." A similar phenomenon occurred in government a few years ago with respect to the cost-overrun problem in industrial contracts. Accountants who brought the issue into focus often found themselves relieved of their assignments, and some were even subject to more severe treatment.

This phenomenon can also be seen in academic institutions. A professor who persists in advocating a deviant point of view is likely to receive fewer promotions and at a slower rate than more "cooperative" colleagues. Indeed, the origins of tenure—guaranteeing a professor continuity of employment without regard for the positions advocated—demonstrate how, in the history of academic institutions, efforts have been made to protect people with different points of view from the inappropriate exercise of pressures to conform.

Group Pressure and Compliance

Because adverse consequences may be the penalty for expressing "deviant" convictions, people may hide their true feelings and express those that support the group norm. A case similar to that of Johnny Rocco was used to study participant judgments, with a seven-point scale marking their reactions on how to deal with a student. After their initial reactions they were given data that led them to believe the majority of the group took a position different from theirs. This study shows greater convergence when a group member believes that his or her opinion will be made public than when it is to be kept private. In addition, there is greater convergence if the member believes that there is a possibility of rejection from the group. The results suggest that anticipated group pressures act on a person as though they were real.[4]

Much is known about outer compliance with norms that hides inner rejection of those norms. This is important—it is called "lip service."[5] When leaders mistake lip service for inward commitment, it is easy to misread the situation. This happens, for example, when management believes a union election will go one way (the way management wants it to go), but in fact it goes the other way—because employees had been showing outer compliance to a position that management wanted to hear but that they inwardly rejected. The only known antidote to this problem is to give those whose behavior is regulated by norms the opportunity to participate in open and candid discussions in which they can voice private attitudes. Such discussions can bring about a congruence between inward belief and outward compliance.

Once a group has converged and a norm has been established, conformity pressures keep the norm in use. In many respects, this is basic to the exercise of cooperation. The major limitations are that the basis of cooperation may no longer be in tune with the needs of the time and inner attitudes may not support "lip service" conformity.

The implication of this for productivity is evident. Once a norm of productivity is established, it is extremely difficult to raise it by ordinary approaches to supervision. Asking a group leader who does not understand the role of productivity norms to get subordinates to work harder will do little to bring about improvements in productivity. Adding productivity rewards is also unlikely to bring about a constructive change. Trying to be persuasive by pleading how important productivity is to the corporation is unlikely to produce more than momentary benefits. Picking out one member who is prepared to break the norm and go above the group level will only cause that person to be seen as a deviant. It may even produce a backlash of lowered productivity by the group as a whole. When the productivity norm is anchored in group attitudes, the elevation of productivity is a realistic possibility only if supervisors understand the dynamics of convergence, cohesion, and conformity pressures.

NOTES

1. J. P. Wright, *On a Clear Day You Can See General Motors*. New York: Avon Books, 1979.

2. The study by Schachter of conformity, deviation, and rejection, using the Johnny Rocco case, demonstrates that communication to the deviant is followed by rejection when he or she continues to deviate. See S. Schachter, "Deviation, Rejection, and Communication," *Journal of Abnormal and Social Psychology*, 1951, *46:* 190–207.

3. Other studies demonstrate that this finding holds true not only when opinions differ from those of the majority but also when abilities are out of line or when emotions are different. See B. Latane, ed., "Studies in Social Comparison," *Journal of Experimental and Social Psychology*, Supplement 1, 1966; and S. Schachter, *The Psychology of Affiliation*. Stanford, Cal.: Stanford University Press, 1959. The Schachter study is replicated in R. M. Emerson, "Deviation and Rejection: An Experimental Replication," *American Sociological Review*, 1954, *19:* 688–693.

An important extension is found in J. M. Levine, L. Saxe, and H. J. Harris, "Reaction to Attitude Deviance: Impact of Deviate's Direction and Distance of Movement." *Sociometry*, 1976, *39*(2): 97–107.

4. See B. H. Raven, "Social Influence on Opinions and the Communication of Related Content," *Journal of Abnormal and Social Psychology*, 1959, *58*(1): 119–128.

5. A study by Schachter (S. Schachter and R. Hall, "Group-Derived Restraints and Audience Persuasion," *Human Relations*, 1952, *5:* 397–406) demonstrates one of the dynamics of "lip service" conformity. Members of university classes were asked if they would participate in a psychological experiment to take place in six weeks. In some instances a false majority accepting the request was instructed beforehand to raise its hands. The rate of volunteering of those who were not instructed was significantly higher when they saw others around them volunteering than when volunteering meant having to stand out as different from the rest of one's classmates. However, six weeks later, when people were expected to appear, those who volunteered because they had seen many others doing so often did not show

up. The likelihood of people following through on their commitment was greatest when that commitment was given in opposition to what other people were doing.

The issue of private acceptance and public conformity is discussed in detail in C. A. Kiesler and S. B. Kiesler, *Conformity*. Reading, Pa.: Addison-Wesley, 1969, pp. 62–87.

A study by Gerard also demonstrates the problem of public compliance and private rejection when group pressure is removed. In his experiments subjects voiced opinions similar to those around them. In a later setting, they were asked to argue for their group's point of view. The confederate was trained to argue effectively against various group positions, particularly against the consensus reached in the subject's former group. Those people who changed their opinions as a result of attack were the ones who were less attracted to their group. This result provides some basis for understanding the issue of private endorsement or lack of endorsement of a norm. See H. B. Gerard, "The Anchorage of Opinions in Face-to-Face Groups," *Human Relations*, 1954, 7: 313–325.

6
Maintaining Independence

We have seen that the dynamics operating in most group situations create pressures toward unanimity. Furthermore, we have come to recognize that these pressures can ride roughshod over sound thinking that challenges group agreement. It is possible to arrive at a position or norm without thinking it through, without examining divergent points of view for creative approaches. We also know that sometimes people who privately disagree with others go along in public and conform to the group's expressed views.

We can now examine the situation experienced by the person who advocates a point of view different from that of the group norm and compare it with that of the person who agrees publicly with the group norm but has private reservations. How are conformity pressures experienced by a person who seems naturally to disagree with others? This is the situation that applies when one person wants to be more productive but is aware that working more productively might make him or her a deviant in the eyes of fellow workers.

52

Independence of Thought

How people try to retain their independence has been investigated experimentally.[1] A situation is created in which what one person perceives as physical reality is contradicted by others, who report seeing physical reality quite differently. Depending on the particular variation of the experiment, from seven to nine people convene to make visual judgments of the lengths of lines projected on a wall in front of them. Three different lines—A, B, and C—are presented and compared with D, a standard line. The three lines are of different lengths, but one of them is the same length as the standard line D. Sometimes A, B, and C are all close to the same length, making judgment more difficult, and sometimes they are vastly different, making judgment easy. When a person experiences this judgment situation alone, the matching accuracy is close to 100 percent, proving that the discrimination is well within the capacity of people making objective judgments on their own.

The key participant, whose judgments are the object of study, is the last person to report. Those reporting before him or her have all been instructed to give the same answer. On some trials, the answer of the others is correct. On other trials it is incorrect—that is, the line they report as matching the standard is not the right one.

The last person to report is uninstructed, a free agent. If independence is maintained by the last person, he or she contradicts the incorrect reports of those responding before and gives the right answer publicly. However, as many as a third to a half of the participants do not retain their independence and do not report according to the evidence of their eyes. Rather, they yield to the social reality and agree with those who gave incorrect answers.

How do those who yield and agree with the incorrect report of the others account for their behavior when interviewed on completion of the experiment? Do they feel they have been hoodwinked? No. They fail to penetrate the contrived nature of the situation. Some deny the evidence of their own eyes, protesting that the other participants were correct and they themselves actually perceived the lines just as the others responded. Some feel uneasy because they realize they are unable to account for the contradiction between what they saw and what others reported.

How do those who retain their independence feel upon being interviewed? They feel rewarded, satisfied with themselves for having stood their ground and having reported their perceptions even when they disagreed with others.

This experiment shows that many of us prefer to resolve potential disagreement by agreeing with others, even when the price of this agreement is the distortion of physical reality. The attitude is, "How could I be right when the majority is seeing something different from what I see? I must be wrong. Therefore, if I want the acceptance of the majority, I had better shift to its point of view."

The conclusions reached in this visual experiment can be reviewed with the Johnny Rocco study presented in the preceding chapter. The first shows the existence of conformity pressures from the group and demonstrates that groups are intolerant of people who hold deviant positions. The second shows how an individual reacts to conformity pressures and demonstrates that many people prefer to be like others even when this means they have to yield. In a group situation each of these forces tends to move members toward agreeing with one another, toward embracing shared norms, and toward avoiding positions that would result in losing membership in the group.

All of these forces are understandable. They are the recognized ways in which norms become established. Once established, norms become the basis of coordination and cooperation. Because people share a norm, each person can anticipate that others will act in a like-minded manner. If and when a deviant appears, effort is concentrated on bringing that person back into line. Continued resistance (independence) carries the risk of rejection.

The conclusion that we are led to is that norms and standards have overriding importance in organizational life, whether the norms are formal and explicit or informal and implicit. We know intuitively the importance of staying in line, and yet it is self-evident that norms and standards can become outmoded. Ultimately they can become significant barriers to progress and change, and if no one can challenge them, there is little hope for change and progress.

Now let's turn to the quality and importance of independent thinking. Although, as we have seen, many people accede to group pressure if only for the sake of acceptance and harmony, some people hold to their opinions and are even willing to be ostracized to prove the validity of their thinking.

This is one of the important means of bringing about innovation and change when the prevailing norm is outmoded. History gives us many examples of people who have been able to maintain their independence successfully under pressure to conform and have changed the way the world thinks. Darwin comes to mind as an important illustration; so does Marx. The leaders of all revolutions are ipso facto nonconformists. The successful ones set entirely new directions for their country; the unsuccessful ones planted seeds that cannot be ignored. Other, less dramatic, examples exist in abundance, but they are unheralded because the changes they brought about were of a lesser magnitude.

How can people be strengthened to maintain a position or to argue for a point of view that is different from the prevailing norm? To answer this question, we must first examine the characteristics of people that relate to their readiness to take an independent position. Then we can study the characteristics of group interaction that foster the expression of divergent viewpoints.

Factors Affecting Degree of Independence

It is clear from research on conformity that there are individual differences in susceptibility to group pressures. A person is more susceptible to influence from others when he or she has failed at a previous task,[2] has been ridiculed or embarrassed,[3] or has deviated from others' opinions or attitudes on a previous issue.[4] People low in self-esteem are more likely to go along with a majority point of view with which they disagree than people whose self-esteem is higher.[5] The same holds for competence. A person of low competence is more likely to conform than a person of high competence.[6] A person is also more susceptible to another's influence when the other person is of higher status or prestige.[7]

Now we can turn to factors in the group that increase the readiness of an individual to express or maintain an independent point of view.

One condition conducive to independence of expression is anonymity. People are more likely to express a divergent point of view when they cannot be pinned down and when sanctions cannot be brought to bear for an unpopular position.[8] This explains the success of the "suggestion box" approach to eliciting new solutions to old problems. By asking people to state their ideas anonymously, you are keeping the evidence of their criticism or deviant thinking from public examination.

When someone who holds a different position from that of the group finds support by even *one* other member, the effects of group pressure are significantly reduced.[9] This is true no matter how unified the others may be. The presence of an ally is sufficient to give the independent person the support necessary for clinging to his or her ideas and arguing for them until fuller examination can lead to a sound basis for acceptance or rejection. The ally may be another person who shares the same view or even someone who has not made up his or her mind and serves merely to break the unanimity of opposition.

The importance of the ally is revealed in other ways. When the ally initially gives support but then decides to join the majority, the readiness of the independent person to throw in the towel increases. If the person who is maintaining independence is resisted by a solid wall of opponents and one of the opponents decides to join him or her, that person is significantly strengthened and is likely to persist. Thus we see the importance of one other person giving support to the person seeking to maintain independence.[10]

We can presume that everyone has an intuitive understanding of the value of independence. We see this in the acceptance of the classic role of devil's advocate. A devil's advocate is one who seeks to promote examination of an alternative point of view but does not take personal responsibility for it. It is an "iffy" support of an independent position rather than a genuine one. Even though weakened by their hypothetical quality, the arguments of the devil's advocate undoubtedly serve to challenge the status quo and stimulate expression of divergent points of view that may lead to innovative solutions.

The devil's advocate can also help a person seeking to maintain independence by standing with him or her. The weakness of this approach, of course, is that the position taken by the devil's advocate is, by definition, not reliable. This is evident in the very language itself: advocating the "devil's" point of view implies that there is something wicked and negative about the independent position, even before it is considered.

From a consultant's point of view, the following has frequently been observed as a key explanation for the capacity of some people to exercise leadership of exceptionally high quality and to lead others in new and uncharted ways rather than merely to keep an ongoing system running smoothly. We observe these people and marvel at how they can challenge others, go against prevailing opinions, and be correct over such a long period.

On deeper examination we discover that almost every great leader of this sort has enjoyed the support of a confidant, someone to whom he or she can expose the incompleteness of his or her thinking, the sound and the unsound alike. A confidant accepts whatever is offered, not in a blind or obedient way, but rather from the standpoint of offering constructive criticism and support when doubts are strong, giving reactions that can be trusted, and then receding into the background when conclusions have been reached.

We know far less about the role of the confidant than we would like, but we know enough to assume that one is almost always present in the upper reaches of management. Consultants routinely enter situations on the premise that there is a confidant to the president. It is rare that study has failed to identify one. The president's confidant may be internal—that is, a subordinate executive in whom the president has complete trust and therefore feels free to expose his or her thinking to full review. Or the confidant may be an outsider, perhaps from the legal profession, a person whose trustworthiness has been demonstrated in past encounters and who therefore can be relied upon to give the kind of objective support that a leader needs when searching for the solution to complex matters. Quite often the confidant is the chief executive's partner in marriage.

Many people of lesser organizational rank also enjoy this kind of support in their efforts to maintain independence. Managers may talk to their spouses or have friends, either within the company or outside it, to whom they can turn when confronted with opposition in order to gain the needed support for thinking through difficult situations. It is not only top leaders who benefit from sharing their problems with the confidant; it is people at every level of the organization.

Recognizing that many people share their corporate or work problems with their marriage partner or friends, we may then raise the question, "Is an internal confidant better than someone external to the immediate situation?" The advantage of an insider as confidant is that the insider is likely to know more of the subtleties of the situation. The disadvantage is that the insider is operating under the same pressures as the person seeking to maintain independence. As a result, such a confidant poses certain difficulties to the person seeking to maintain independence. The confidant, sensing some personal risk in such an alliance, may feel somewhat compromised by the situation. Or, perhaps because of some divided loyalties, the confidant may not be entirely objective. But even with such limitations, the presence of a confidant is very supportive.

There is one more type of independent person to include in this review. Research on creativity reveals that some people seem to be natural antagonists. They reject the prevailing point of view, almost without regard for what it is.[11] Furthermore, they seem to seek out points of disagreement and ally themselves with the unpopular side of controversies. Such people have been described in a variety of ways, but for our purposes we can say that they are "structural deviants." They simply approach situations with the idea of not "buying" the popular point of view.

Structural deviants may contribute great benefits as a result of the challenges they put forward, but they are using an unpopular way to bring about innovations. Such people are constantly on the margin of social acceptance and often fail to benefit in terms consistent with the contribution that their opposition provides. Structural deviants are usually unaware of their need to be different. They frequently find themselves trapped into controversies when originally they had no intention of taking a partisan position.

Independence and Group Interaction

Now that we have examined some of the factors that affect the way people behave, both in maintaining their independence and in conforming to group pressures, we should examine the dynamics of group interaction. When these dynamics are understood, we can sharpen our skills in using them as a creative approach to solving problems through teamwork and group activity. Then norms that would otherwise lead to convergence or conformity pressures can be utilized to free people. With a fuller comprehension of group dynamics, we are in a position to increase the readiness of others to express a divergent point of view.

When a person is seen to be resisting pressure to conform, any one of us is in a position to offer the kind of support necessary for ensuring that the person's position is examined rather than summarily rejected or overridden. This is not difficult to do. It entails being ready to say, "Wait a minute. Bill is trying to make a point, and we're not giving him the opportunity to express himself. Let's back off and listen and see if we can understand why Bill is promoting that position. We may all be able to learn something."

When people face a wall of opposition, it is difficult for them to retain independence, even when their position is a valid one. People need self-confidence and high self-esteem to maintain independence under those circumstances.

Given that maintaining group membership while resisting group pressures constitutes a dilemma, we can recognize the importance of taking suitable action to reduce the pressures to conform in order to avoid the harmful effects of holding on to outmoded norms.

NOTES

1. S. E. Asch, "Effects of Group Pressure upon the Modification and Distortion of Judgment," in H. Guetzkow, ed., *Groups, Leadership, and Men.* Pittsburgh: Carnegie Press, 1951. See also R. A. Crutchfield, "Assessments of Persons Through a Quasi Group-Interaction Technique," *Journal of Abnormal and Social Psychology,* 1951, *46:* 577–588.

2. H. C. Kelman, "Effects of Success and Failure on Suggestibility in the Autokinetic Situation," *Journal of Abnormal and Social Psychology,* 1950, *45:* 267–285.

3. In a study by Duval, subjects were told that in terms of their attitudes they were similar to 95 percent, about the same as 50 percent, or similar to only 5 percent of a normative group. Thereafter, they were exposed to live images of themselves on a television monitor to create an embarrassing situation. The holding of unusual attitudes—that is, like only 5 percent of the others—in the presence of the TV monitoring increased conformity. See S. Duval, "Conformity on a Visual Task as a Function of Personal Novelty on Attitude Dimensions and Being Reminded of the Object's State Itself," *Journal of Experimental Social Psychology,* 1976, *12:* 87–93. Also see R. Apsler, "Effects of Embarrassment on Behavior Toward Others," *Journal of Personality and Social Psychology,* 1975, *32*(1): 145–153; T. A. Filter and A. E. Gross, "Effects of Public and Private Deviancy on Compliance with a Request," *Journal of Experimental and Social Psychology,* 1975, *11:* 553–559; and C. M. Steel, "Name-Calling and Compliance," *Journal of Personality and Social Psychology,* 1975, *31:* 361–369.

4. J. M. Darley, T. Moriarity, and E. Berscheid, "Increased Conformity to a Fellow Deviant as a Function of Prior Deviation," *Journal of Experimental Social Psychology,* 1974, *10:* 211–223. In a two-part experiment, people who had the experience of deviating from the majority on one task tended to conform more on a second task. This suggests that the individual is influenced by the experience of being different.

5. D. J. Stand, "Conformity, Ability, and Self-Esteem," *Representative Research in Social Psychology,* 1972, *3*(1): 97–103.

6. Those who feel very competent on a particular task are unlikely to conform to the group because for them the social influence and the information that the group holds are relatively weak sources of reality in comparison with their own experience. See D. L. Wiesenthal, N. S. Endler, T. R. Coward, and J. Edwards, "Reversibility of Relative Competence as a Determinant of Conformity Across Different Perceptual Tasks," *Representative Research in Social Psychology,* 1976, *7:* 35–43.

7. D. L. Cole, "The Influence of Task Perception and Leader Variation on Autokinetic Responses," *American Psychologist,* 1955, *10:* 343 (abstract).
·

8. M. Deutsch and H. Gerard, "A Study of Normative and Informational Social Influences upon Individual Judgment," *Journal of Abnormal and Social Psychology*, 1955, *51*(1): 629–636.

9. The presence of an ally, even one who is not seen to give valid judgments, is enough to reduce the amount of conformity significantly. In a study involving judgment of visual stimuli, such as length of lines, subjects were given an ally under two of three conditions. Under the third condition they were given no ally and faced uniform disagreement with their position. In one circumstance the ally had thick glasses and was presumed to be unable to see what he was judging. Even so, conformity was less than when the subject had no ally. However, when the ally did not wear glasses and was believed to have good sight, he induced a significantly greater amount of independence than when the ally was presumed to be almost blind. This means that an ally reduces conformity significantly, but an ally upon whom one can rely does so to an even greater degree. See V. L. Allen and J. M. Levine, "Social Support and Conformity: The Role of Independent Assessment of Reality," *Journal of Experimental Social Psychology*, 1971, 7: 48–58.

An excellent analysis of the greater confidence-reducing impact on a naive majority of two deviants in a face-to-face group who are consistent with one another and over a series of judgments in comparison with a lone deviant is provided in S. Moscovici and E. Lage, "Studies in Social Influence III: Majority Versus Minority Influence in a Group," *European Journal of Social Psychology*, 1976, *6*(2): pp. 149–174.

10. S. E. Asch, "Effects of Group Pressure upon the Modification and Distortion of Judgment," in H. Guetzkow, ed., *Groups, Leadership, and Men.* Pittsburgh: Carnegie Press, 1951.

11. Ivor Morrish, *Aspects of Educational Change.* New York: Wiley, 1976, pp. 98–102. Morrish describes the characteristics of "innovators," those who are opposed on principle to the present order of things but who have nothing particularly solid to support their position. They are against the status quo and are rarely particularly popular people. Personality characteristics of such innovators have been studied by O. Harvey, "Conceptual Systems in Attitude Change," in C. Sherif and M. Sherif, *Attitude, Ego, Involvement, and Change.* New York: Wiley, 1967, pp. 201–226; M. B. Miles, "On Temporary Systems," in M. B. Miles, ed., *Innovation in Education.* New York: Teachers College Press, Columbia University, 1964, pp. 37–92; E. Katz, "Diffusion of New Ideas and Practices," in W. Schramm, ed., *The Science of Human Communications: New Directions and New Findings in Communication Research.* New York: Basic Books, 1963; and E. M. Rogers, "What Are Innovators Like?" in R. O. Carlson et al., *Change Processes in the Public Schools.* Eugene, Ore.: University of Oregon Press, 1965, pp. 56–61. Innovators were seen as people who have faith in their own evaluation of experience. They also have a sense of personal competence, a high task orientation, and a strong desire to seek information, and they exhibit risk-taking and independent behavior.

7
Intergroup Relationships

So far, our discussion of the dynamics that operate within groups has stopped short of looking at the influences that act on that group from the outside. Let us now see what happens to a group, as an entity, as it functions in the real world and goes about its business, whatever that business is. Very few groups operate in isolation from other groups; therefore, it is important to understand how outside influences affect a group's internal dynamics. What bearing do those influences have on the factors we have been considering—convergence, conformity, cohesion, retention of independence, and so on? A few examples of real-life situations follows.

What goes on in the maintenance group in a manufacturing plant can have a striking effect on how well or how poorly the operations department carries out its responsibilities. The same is true of the relationship between marketing and manufacturing. How each operates affects the other in significant ways. The interaction between union and management groups is of importance in this same sense.

In a university, too, what happens in one department affects other departments, although here the strongest influence is between departments that have some relationship to each other. Thus the department of psychology may be influenced in its internal operations by decisions made within the department of educational psychology; applied mathematics may be influenced by what is going on in pure mathematics; physics may be influenced by developments in chemistry; and so on. Comparable influences exist in a hospital, such as between nursing and food services, between the laboratory and nursing, and between the medical services and administrative organization.

Intergroup Conflict

Three sets of circumstances are important for understanding intergroup conflict. One is when two groups are competing for scarce resources. This happens when the budget is insufficient to meet what are thought to be the legitimate requirements of both groups. The result is that one group gains an advantage over the other if it can get a larger budget. The second is when two groups can function at optimum level only when each anticipates the needs of the other. If one fails to provide the support expected and the other has no basis for understanding why, frustration and antagonism are likely to result. The third is when one group has power over the other and exerts its control in a way that violates the second group's expectations as to what constitutes legitimate control.

In terms of their impact on a group's internal dynamics, we can regard these three situations as essentially the same, because all lead to intergroup competitiveness and antagonism.

The behavioral science research concerned with antagonisms between groups is rich and extensive. Without detailing the mechanics of the research, we will cite some of the conclusions drawn from it. From the standpoint of convergence, conformity, cohesion, and the retention of independence, the following generalizations may be made about intergroup competition.

1. Feelings of competition produce greater readiness to converge toward common norms and attitudes. These norms and attitudes become narrower than when competition is absent, meaning that individual differences are tolerated less.

2. If a person departs from prevailing norms and attitudes, he or she is subject to more intense conformity pressures than would exist in the absence of competition.

3. Cohesion is greater in the presence of competition.

4. A representative of a group is obligated to speak for the group's position by showing loyalty to it. When the representative does so and is able to bring gain back to the group, he or she is seen as a hero. If the representative fails to act loyally, the group reaction is that it is harboring a traitor.

5. Cohesion is retained and may become artificial in the victorious group; it diminishes in the defeated group. The result is infighting.

6. The victorious group retains the norms and attitudes that characterized it during the competition period. It becomes "fat and happy."

7. The defeated group challenges the norms and attitudes that prevailed within it during the period of competition and tries doing things differently. It becomes "lean and hungry."

8. In the victorious group, members feel an even greater need to support positions that have brought them victory.

9. Group members of the defeated group feel less compulsion to adhere to the group's point of view. Therefore, the member is freer to voice his or her thoughts without being seen as a deviant.

We see, then, that competition between two groups for scarce resources, antagonisms produced by one group withholding needed support from another, and the illegitimate exertion of power can have very strong internal effects on a group.

The Dynamics of Competition

The dynamics described above can be seen on a much larger canvas. Let's view them in the context of what occurred between nations during and after World War II. The war produced a coming together, a sense of unity, with shared norms and attitudes both in the countries that constituted the Axis and in those that represented the Allies. The competition between the two sides was vicious. It was win-lose to the end.

The victorious groups were the United States and Great Britain. The defeated groups were Germany, Italy, and Japan. The Soviet Union was somewhere in between, because although it had been allied with the winning side, 20 million Soviet lives were lost and the land was devastated. The task of rebuilding to preeminence was truly gargantuan. The Soviet Union took on the lean and hungry attitude commonly associated with defeat, and has acted consistent with that attitude up to the present.

In the postwar era, the victorious groups appear to have consolidated the norms and standards that brought them their massive victory. Leadership consolidation is seen in the stature afforded wartime military leaders such as George Marshall and Douglas MacArthur. The election of

Dwight D. Eisenhower to the U.S. presidency and the return of Winston Churchill as prime minister of Great Britain are further examples. These nations, in a real sense, became "fat, happy, and complacent." Taking the license of telescoping both time and events, we find that the results are decelerated productivity, reduced creativity, and many social ills. Both countries have entered an extended period of ennui.

The defeated nations—Germany, Italy, and Japan—have played out the pattern characteristic of defeated groups. After the war ended, a period of demoralization lasting several years ensued. There arose a national self-examination as to why things had gone wrong, along with the development of norms and attitudes of "never again." The Marshall Plan and similar programs of economic assistance eventually made it possible for these countries to rebuild. The development of new norms and attitudes fostered impressive records of productivity and creativity that have continued up to the present in both Germany and Japan. Italy is an exception; the reasons are outside the scope of this review.

Similar contrasts can be made in studying the competition between companies and between various industries— for example, that between Sears and Penney or between Kodak and Polaroid. Thus we see that the norms a group develops to regulate conduct within itself may be influenced significantly by outside factors.

How can we turn our understanding of the way norms operate to our advantage? If we become alert to what is going on inside the organization—how groups form and become cohesive, who the leaders of the group are, and who the "deviants" are—we can focus our attention on the norms themselves to see how we can uproot those that are outmoded. We do well to keep before us the example provided by the American automobile manufacturers,[2] who failed to compete in the fuel-efficient compact car field in spite of the developing evidence of the popularity of small vehicles, which became apparent in 1965 and steadily built up to 1980, when small foreign cars captured around 30 percent of the market.

NOTES

1. M. Sherif and C. W. Sherif, *Groups in Harmony Intention.* New York: Harper Bros., 1953. See also M. Sherif, O. J. Harvey, B. J. White, W. R. Hood, and C. W. Sherif, *Intergroup Cooperation and Competition: The Robber's Cave Experiment.* Norman, Okla.: The University Book Exchange, 1961. Also see R. R. Blake and J. S. Mouton, "Reactions to Intergroup Competition Under Win-Lose Conditions," *Management Science,* 1961, 7: 420–435; and R. R. Blake and J. S. Mouton, "The Intergroup Dynamics of Win-Lose Conflict and Problem-Solving Collaboration in Union–Management Relations," in M. Sherif, ed., *Intergroup Relations in Leadership.* New York: Wiley, 1961.

2. This is discussed in detail in J. P. Wright, *On a Clear Day You Can See General Motors.* New York: Avon Books, 1979.

8
Changing Norms to Improve Productivity

There are three reasons for managers in industry, government, and elsewhere to acquire a knowledge of behavioral science. One is to launch new efforts at group leadership in terms consistent with what we know about how and why people behave as they do. In this way managers can avoid creating problems that will have to be lived with or solved at a later time. A second is to gain insight into why some things are going well in order to be able to maintain an established effort at a high level of effectiveness. A third is to gain insight into existing problems that are barriers to effectiveness. Behavioral science knowledge related to norms and to individual attitudes anchored in existing norms is useful in all three of these ways, but its primary value is helping to solve current problems.

Primary and Reference Groups

Two kinds of group membership have comparable effects on an individual from the standpoint of the norms of thought, attitude, and conduct that they shape: primary group membership and reference group membership.

Primary Groups

A primary group is a face-to-face membership group in which people know, at least intuitively, the norms that govern the conduct of each member. Primary group members are frequently in contact with one another and stand ready to enforce norms.

For all practical purposes, it can be said that every employed person has this kind of membership grouping. Every boss has one or more subordinates. This grouping of boss and subordinates constitutes a primary group. Most people are subject to regulation by bosses and subordinates, not only through the direct exercise of power and authority, but also through the operation of norms and standards. This exercise of influence by colleagues is also a significant force in guiding one's on-the-job actions and inactions.

Reference Groups

A reference group is any recognizable organization that in itself can be characterized as having norms and standards. A reference group is unlikely to bring all its members together to meet face to face as a single entity, though members may be in contact with one another. In fact, a person doesn't even need to have a direct membership in a reference group to be subject to regulation by the norms and standards that characterize it. All a person needs is an identification with it—a feeling of pull on positive emotions toward the group. This sense of belonging may exist even if the feeling is private and not backed up by any explicit participation.

One such group is the student body of a comparatively small college—a group that is large enough to make it almost impossible for all students and staff to know one another personally but small enough to have clear-cut identity. The power of reference groups to influence individual attitudes in such a setting was demonstrated in a study of Bennington College. Students from relatively conservative families became increasingly liberal each year they were in school. The underclassmen tended to conform to the opinions of the most popular upperclassmen, and these in-group leaders were relatively liberal in their views.

Another example of a reference group is a professional society. The American Medical Association is an important reference group for medical personnel, though the very people who are influenced by it may not attend any of its meetings. Norms and standards promulgated by the American Medical Association have a strong influence on medical people independent of their active or explicit participation in it. The same is true, of course, for any professional society. Academic personnel characteristically belong to professional societies, and from these professional societies norms and standards emerge for what constitutes sound and effective behavior. An academic person may never leave the campus, but he or she may, through association with others on the campus, or even through reading the journals and magazines of the relevant professional society, be strongly influenced by the norms and standards that characterize the society.

Translated into organizational terms, it can be said that the great majority of employed people see their organization as a reference group. For example, if the company has established a tradition of fair dealings with customers, all its employees are guided by this tradition and will tend to pursue fair dealings when representing the company. The same is true for organizations that have developed a reputation for sleaziness or slippery deals. Then a norm or a standard prevails that "authorizes" employees to take an unfair advantage of clients and others whenever they represent the company. Such actions may be taken independently of supervision.

The following summary identifies the important propositions that have been introduced up to now with respect to either primary or reference groups.

1. When two or more people gather and share their thoughts, attitudes, or feelings, or do not gather but take one another's thoughts, feelings, and attitudes into account, their viewpoints tend to converge. Once such convergence occurs, it takes on the character of a norm.
2. When a norm has been established, group members feel the need to conform to it.
3. Any indication that a member is departing from a norm is likely to cause others to exercise pressure to bring him or her back into line.
4. The member who persists in deviating from a norm runs the risk of isolation and rejection.
5. Since norms are widespread, they have a significantly controlling effect on what people in organizations do and do not do. This influence is exerted independently of what bosses may direct or expect.
6. Even though norms may become outmoded or out of tune with what is needed, they continue to control individuals.

Resistance to Change

Although most people are unaware of the powerful influence that norms exert in regulating behavior, they are aware of the negative feelings aroused by people who do not do things the way they obviously should. We may acknowledge the presence of norms but still not be clear about the factors that cause us to do things the way we do. We may simply be out of touch with them.

As a result of such social blindness, managers who want to change behavior often disregard the existence of norms and rely on the exercise of unilateral power to compel shifts in behavior even when these are resisted. A boss may say to a subordinate, "Shape up or ship out." This statement rests on the assumption that the command itself is strong enough to produce the desired behavior.

The strategy of changing behavior by "decree" is seen in the "a new boss sweeps clean" approach. A new boss takes over a job, sees things not to his or her liking, imposes his or her will on the situation, and tells people in a direct way to stop doing what they have been doing and to start doing what he or she wants done. The boss is using power and authority to break up prevailing norms. This method is sometimes successful, but far more often it fails.

Those whose behavior is expected to shift resist. Though they themselves may not recognize that fact, they prefer to act in accordance with the prevailing norms that are held in place by the influence of colleagues rather than to follow a boss's directives. More often than not, they simply use passive resistance, although sometimes the resistance goes underground. Eventually the new boss comes to terms with it by recognizing his or her inability to introduce change at a rapid rate. Resistance to change has set in. Productivity remains at about the same level as before.

Relying on power and authority to change norms can be risky. Over and above the resistance it provokes, whether active or passive, there is the likelihood of alienating those who are expected to shift their behavior. These people may become resentful and even vengeful. Significantly lowered morale may make it even more difficult to realize the sought-after improvements.

Many bosses in a new assignment realize that their power and authority are weak, or perhaps they sense the adverse consequences that can arise from resistance to change. What do they do under these circumstances? Perhaps we might gain some understanding of the forces that operate by looking at another setting.

Commonly held norms and values make a group less susceptible to disruption from external forces. In an experiment with a group of children who had established ways of playing with toys, an older child who was a leader in another group was introduced as a new member of the group. The new child, in order to be effective, had to learn to act within the constraints of the new group, even though he was more of a leader than the other members. In order to be effective, the child had to learn the "rules" and then find ways to introduce his own modifications in order to exert influence on the other members of the group.[2]

Managers in a new assignment may seek to exert influence but do little more to make their influence felt than change job titles or add a little bit of office decoration. The takeover is symbolic. Such a boss may wait several months until he or she has learned the ropes before trying to introduce real changes. The "go slow" boss learns the norms and standards that prevailed before attempting to introduce changes. However, the boss is more than likely to adopt the prevailing norms and standards. The result is that he or she becomes the spokesman for the normative culture of the group, and ultimately becomes part of it without exerting further influence on the group thereafter.

An alternative to exercising power and authority to command change is to use the knowledge we now have of norms and their influence on behavior to moderate behavior change. This approach will be illustrated in case studies in the next several chapters. First, however, the basic outline of the strategy is presented.

A Strategy for Changing Norms

The way to change norms is to involve those whose behavior is regulated by them in studying what the existing norms are and exploring alternatives that might serve corporate objectives better.[3] Only after prevailing norms are understood can specific steps necessary for shifting from the old to the new be considered and implemented. The key factor is to involve those who are controlled by a norm to change the norm itself. When the norm is shifted, altered attitudes and behavior consistent with the new attitudes can be expected to emerge. The following conditions are basic to success.

1. All norms carriers actively participate. Both primary and reference group members who are carriers of the prevailing norm must actively participate, because it is their support of new patterns of behavior or new norms of productivity (volume, quality, control of waste, and so on) that governs whether new approaches will prevail. Those who are expected to change behavior need the opportunity to experience and become explicit about the prevailing norm and to convince themselves of its soundness or of the need to change. They also need to identify what the new norm should be and to become committed to bringing it into existence. Participation should include all primary group members. The reason is that they may be crucial to giving the okay to change. If they are not a part of the change effort, chances are they won't support it.

In addition, reference group members whose leadership exerts an influence on the organizational culture may participate even if they are only indirectly concerned with the norm in question. Their explicit support of the new norm adds positive force to the change. The absence of their expressed support is likely to have a dampening effect on those whose behavior the norm regulates. An example in the union–management area is the foreman, who is often in the most direct contact with the union. However, foremen, as members of the larger reference group of management, are unlikely to shift attitudes without a corresponding change throughout management.

2. Leadership is by those responsible for ultimate decisions. There is no realistic prospect for changing norms and standards if those who are the leaders of the prevailing norm system absent themselves from the effort. The reason is obvious. If they do not think through the prevailing norms and the limitations in behavior that these create, they are in no position to give their leadership approval or the identification and development of new and more appropriate norms.

Failure to involve the leaders is the inherent weakness in conventional quality of work life (QWL) and quality circle (QC) approaches to change. It is not overcome by the use of trained leaders who are themselves not a part of the primary membership group. In a study[4] of the effect of leader presence versus leader absence on shifting the norms regarding group problem solving, six natural teams—those who comprised a work group—engaged in a one-week study of interpersonal and organizational problems to increase their effectiveness. One of the teams had the boss present. Five others were without a boss. An additional team represented cousins—people who were from the same agency but who had no working relationship in terms of the organizational hierarchy. On a variety of measures before the team study and six months later, only the team that had the boss present made any appreciable change in behavior. The results suggest what a powerful impact the leader has on the success of a change effort and how the absence of the leader, whose behavior and attitudes strongly influence subordinates, makes it difficult, if not impossible, for subordinates to shift their behavior.

3. Participants are involved with the problem. Norms are

likely to be anything but explicit and self-evident. Therefore, the problem is how to identify them so that they can be dealt with in an objective manner. How might participants study a problem in order to discover the norm that regulates how they deal with it? The answer to this question is at the crux of whether or not organization members can learn better management of norms and standards.

One valuable tool for studying problems and discovering norms is the task paragraph.[5] The task paragraph contains two parts. The first part is an open, direct, and unbiased statement that identifies the problem. The second part asks participants what can be done to solve it. The task paragraph, in other words, focuses on the issue at hand, not on the norm presumed to underlie it or on the attitudes that derive from the norm. It avoids psychologizing or making evaluative judgments or suggestions as to causes or solutions. The value of the task paragraph is that it gives clear definition to the problem. Using the task paragraph statement of the problem, those concerned with solving it can then analyze why the problem exists and what can be done to solve it.

Let's use this question as an example of focusing the solution of a problem: "What are the causes of our rampant absenteeism, and what can be done about it?"

When employees at one plant tried to discuss this question, an endless variety of answers were suggested. Nothing seemed to click until one of the participants said, "The real problem is that it has become a way of life. No one wants to maintain a perfect attendance record when each person knows everyone else thinks it's okay to be absent for personal reasons. Since there is no enforcement of any absenteeism policy, people's attitudes have become entrenched."

Others readily agreed, leading to the conclusion that if the true norm that regulated the behavior of individuals had been identified, it was based on a very lax concept of employee responsibility to the company.

Having accomplished the first part—formulating an unbiased statement of the problem—participants can directly address the question of how to change the situation.

We have demonstrated the value of the task paragraph in focusing attention on an examination of the real problem. We have also shown how, once discussion is focused on the real problem, the norm regulating the conduct of many people can become visible. Getting participants involved in diagnosing the problem is the first step. This is not equivalent to describing the norm that exists behind it. Only by clarifying the statement of the problem first is it possible to ask whether the problem is caused by norms or is related to something else.

Take an example introduced in Chapter 1: the adverse impact on productivity caused by people slacking off during the last hour of work. It might be possible to get employees involved in the problem by having them answer this question stated in task paragraph form: "What are the causes of people slacking off during the last hour of the day, and how can the problem be solved?" Also described in Chapter 1 was a chronic and difficult union-management relationship. Involvement in that problem might be achieved by a task paragraph question such as this: "Is it possible to establish a good problem-solving relationship with the union, and what are the consequences of not trying to do so?" The statement of the problem, in other words, clarifies the issue and asks those concerned with it to think about what the causes are and whether they see it as a problem to be solved.

4. Facts and data are provided about the objective situation. Sometimes norms have been based on false information. When this is so, providing participants with objective evidence of the true state of affairs can facilitate the rejection of the old norm and the acceptance of one that squares better with the facts in the situation.

5. Ventilation and catharsis are provided. Those involved in a problem—both employees who practice the unproductive behavior and those who are responsible for it—are often frustrated by its continued existence. They blame others for it. Without the opportunity to get their frustrations and antagonisms into the open, they continue to find it difficult to think constructively about how the problem might be resolved. In these circumstances, it is essential to create an atmosphere that allows those who are a part of the problem to discharge their feelings and emotions. Only in this way is it possible to get the negative attitudes that are preventing constructive problem solving out of the way. Such emotions and feelings constitute evidence that members share a norm, one that they are likely to enforce on one another in a way that makes a deviant suspect.

6. Reasons for the current problem are identified. Participants often have different explanations of a problem. Discussion separates false from valid explanations.

7. Implicit agreements are made explicit. Whatever the discussions produce by way of proposed new attitudes and behaviors, the conclusions that are reached need to be crystallized and validated by public agreement rather than simply presumed to be widely acceptable.

8. Changes in norms are followed up. New norms are always weaker than those they replace. The result is that people tend to backslide toward the norm that previously prevailed. Follow-up is essential to strengthen new attitudes and behavior and bring them into effective use.

These norm-setting strategies are most acceptable when they are consistent with other organizationwide efforts to pursue corporate excellence. In spite of their contribution to productivity, they are likely to be misinterpreted and even resented if carried out in isolation.

With these steps in mind, we are now in a position to examine how changes in norms can bring about behavior change in specific situations. The chapters that follow provide case studies of how systematic knowledge of norms and the attitudes associated with them can be used successfully to solve complex organizational problems.

NOTES

1. T. M. Newcomb, *Personality and Social Change.* New York: Dryden, 1943. These ideological changes that occurred in college persisted a quarter of a century later, as indicated by follow-up studies. See T. M. Newcomb, K. E. Koenig, R. Flacks, and D. P. Warwick, *Persistence in Change: Bennington College and Its Students After Twenty-Five Years.* New York: Wiley, 1967.

2. See F. Merei, "Group Leadership and Institutionalization," *Human Relations,* 1949, *2:* 23–29.

3. The distinction between unilateral and participative approaches to changing norms identifies the 9,1 versus 9,9 orientations in the Managerial Grid. For further reference, see R. R. Blake and J. S. Mouton, *The New Managerial Grid.* Houston: Gulf Publishing Company, 1978, pp. 16–47; and R. R. Blake and J. S. Mouton, *The Versatile Manager: A Grid Profile.* Homewood, Ill.: Dow Jones–Irwin, 1981, pp. 133–143.

4. R. Wayne Boss, "The Effects of Leader Absence on a Confrontational Team-Building Design," *Journal of Applied Behavioral Science,* 1978, *14*(4): 469–478.

5. The specific steps useful for preparation of task paragraphs are provided in J. S. Mouton and R. R. Blake, *Instrumented Team Learning.* Austin, Texas: Scientific Methods, Inc., 1975, pp. 45–51.

9
The Management of Safety

There are a variety of ways to analyze accidents, their causes, and the techniques for preventing accidents or keeping them at a minimum.

One approach centers on accident-proneness. Some people have career records of accidents while others, working under comparable conditions, seem never to have a problem. The difference is within the individual people involved. Therefore, an important part of the management of safety is selection—bringing employees with the maximum likelihood of being able to work in a safe manner into work situations that pose some hazard.

Another approach is to ensure that those who work under conditions of potential risk are adequately protected by safety equipment—goggles when welding or using drilling equipment, hard hats whenever there is a risk of falling objects, gloves when the hands can be hurt, heavy shoes or boots when the feet need to be protected. Safety equipment can significantly cut down the hazards present in many kinds of work.

Still another approach to safety is to make and enforce

safety rules. These rules are expected to be respected by those who are at risk. An area in which walking is risky is marked "Dangerous"; so is an area where heavy equipment is moving and operators may not see pedestrians because they are concentrating on their equipment.

Still another approach to safety focuses on state and federal safety regulations that are applied on an industrywide basis. These are necessary because many companies, each competing with one another, won't implement them unless all do so in a uniform way. The reason, of course, is that if only one were to introduce some of the safety rules, the expense of doing so would make that company noncompetitive. Therefore, it is essential that government regulate on an across-industry basis.

Each of these approaches has an important contribution to make in the overall management of safety, yet none of them can make much of a contribution if employees share attitudes that involve needless risk taking.

Recall the situation described in Chapter 1 in which one plant had the poorest safety record out of 12 sister plants across the nation. One after another of the various approaches to the accident problem had been implemented, but the poor safety record was not corrected. Thus the plant constituted a "natural" location for an experiment along the lines detailed in previous chapters. The experiment was done in the following way.

Statement of the Problem

A task paragraph was produced that clearly stated the problem and then asked, "What is the cause of our poor safety record? How can it be improved?" A total of 800 employees, both supervisory and wage and salaried personnel, participated. The study consisted of two parts: a preparatory segment and a seminar discussion period of eight hours, leading to crystallization of a new safety norm. Seminars consisted of 80 people assembled in leaderless discussion groups of 10. Each seminar was conducted over a two-day period. The ratio of supervisors to wage and salaried personnel in the discussion groups was the same as in the organizational population. No effort was made to put supervisors and those whom they directly supervised in the same groups, but no effect was made to separate them either.

Each seminar commenced after lunch on the first day and continued until the end of the workday. It picked up the morning of the second day and ended at noon. All sessions were conducted in the plant itself. Leaders of the several unions participated, not as union representatives but as employees of the company.

The preparatory work consisted of examining background materials related to previous accidents, with the past 25 lost-time accidents reviewed. The accidents were described and richly illustrated with pictures, the cause(s) identified, and conclusion drawn as to how each problem might have been avoided and how it could be corrected in the future. Participants were expected to study the prework document and to be prepared to discuss the material during the seminars.

The seminars began with a discussion of the question posed in the task paragraph. Even a casual observer would recognize that all participants in the discussions were deeply concerned with the problem. The entire session was serious business. The groups were so comparable that the following description is sufficient to indicate what the discussions entailed.

In group after group, statements made by participants—primarily wage and salaried personnel (although supervisors quickly joined in, once the issue developed)—centered on "them-ism": "The 'real cause' of all these accidents is 'them.' We get pushed for productivity these days in a way that was never true before the new management took over. That's the cause of the problem—pressure.''

Another point of view was, "They don't care. It's not like the old days. It used to be that when any risk was involved, the safety inspector would check it out first. He'd tell us what to do and what not to do. They don't do that any more. As a matter of fact, we used to have 15 safety inspectors and we could call on them any time. Nowadays two people in the personnel department are responsible for safety, and that's it. It's become a line of responsibility and the line doesn't know how to study the situation and really determine what the factors of risk are.''

A third point of view frequently expressed was, "It's the equipment, it's getting old." Still another: "It's the new people. They come in and are not given adequate training. Before you know it, an accident has happened.''

The point here is that the tension people felt from being under pressure and subject to the risk of accidents had produced substantial anger, and a target of these angry reactions was "them"—that is, management.

Emergence of the New Norm

After the catharsis and ventilation period, someone in a group, or occasionally a higher-level manager who was responsible for monitoring the discussions, intervened. Members were asked whether the "explanations" of accidents given by participants squared with the facts of 25 accident synopses examined in the preliminary phase. The prework document had been written to illuminate the reality of the situation and to increase objectivity.

Most participants initially preferred their own explanations to the conclusions from the accident studies. Yet there was enough concern about exploring the problem in greater depth for the synopses of accidents to come to the fore. What the study demonstrated, by and large, was that very few of the accidents could be traced to faulty equipment or to lack of safety rules or safety equipment. More often than not, the accident was the personal responsibility of the employee who had suffered it.

For example, an eye accident that resulted in lost time had happened when an employee was sweating and took his goggles off because of difficulties he was having in seeing the work. An electrical burn resulted when an employee was making a fine adjustment and found it difficult to do so with the heavy gloves on. By taking off his gloves, he placed himself at an increased risk and suffered the burn. Another accident was caused by an employee walking in an area marked "Dangerous" and slipping on grease, with a resultant bone injury.

As the discussion continued through the afternoon of the first day, it became clear that two alternative explanations were under examination. Only one of them could be valid. Either it was the "them" norm, as evidenced in equipment, rules, pressure, and so on, or it was the "us" norm. The accident results clearly indicated that shortcutting and trying to solve a problem by convenience were, far more often than not, suggestive of the real problem.

When the discussions resumed at the beginning of day 2, some of the "them-ism" returned, and a new but far briefer period of catharsis and ventilation was necessary in some groups to get back to a problem-solving orientation.

By the end of the first hour of day 2 most groups had arrived at an entirely different notion than anyone had had at the beginning of the discussions. Typical comments were, "When you come right down to it, it's not them; it's us. We can blame them, but we put ourselves at risk." "We've developed sloppy work habits; we cut corners, not because we have to or because we're pressured to, but because we've become sloppy." "We don't look out for one another. I see you entering an area marked 'Dangerous' when you've got no good reason to be there, and I say nothing. You slip. They didn't cause your broken hip; you and I did."

By this time, the old norm of blaming problems on management and refusing to be personally responsible had become visible and was beginning to crumble. A new norm began to replace it. The new norm might be described in the following way: "We are the last link on the safety chain. You can't blame rules if the rules are okay but we don't follow them. You can't even blame supervisors, though they could do more to chew us out when they see an infraction. You can't blame safety equipment if it's not in place and in use when the accident occurs. We can only take the responsibility for our accident situation ourselves."

Commitment to the New Norm

Translated into practice, the new norm resulted in supervisors and wage and salaried personnel committing themselves to being responsible for themselves and for one another. Each person was committed to adhering to safety practices, and employees who didn't know what the practices were, would ask others for help. All employees agreed on the importance of being mutually responsible. In other words, "I will call your hand, as one employee to another, whenever I see you involved in a foolish action. I expect you to call my hand the same way. If we're the last link on the safety chain, we can solve the problem only by strengthening the link. Being self-responsible and mutually responsible are the only possible ways for strengthening that link."

With all employees whose activities placed them at risk committed to personal and mutual responsibility for safe practices, the poor safety record in the plant was quickly reversed in the 12-plant comparison. The plant rapidly moved up in safety. Within nine months it led the other 11.

The solution the workers reached was based on the readiness of individuals to converge on a norm that squared with experiential reality. Once the strategy of discussion made it possible for the participants themselves to define the problem, the old norm, characterized by "them-ism," was rejected as an unsatisfactory basis of behavior. The new norm of personal and mutual responsibility was quickly implemented and served beautifully to rectify the problem.

10
Reworking
the Union–Management
Relationship

A union–management relationship that had been chroni-
cally bad over the years and recently became inflamed by an
extended strike was introduced in Chapter 1. The corporation engaged in organization development and came to see
many problems in a new light. One was related to this mutually destructive relationship. Let's look at the case in some
detail.

Management of the company had employed a consulting
firm with expertise in union busting. Various strategies were
applied in the effort to destroy the union. The union turned
out to have far greater support from its membership than
management had calculated. Management had routinely
found encouragement when some member reported that
"there were only 15 at the union hall last night." The absence of public participation was misinterpreted as a lack of
private commitment. Management assumed that because
union members failed to attend meetings, they did not truly
support the union's position. This was an inaccurate reading
of the true convictions of union members.

The union-busting tactic did not work. A strike was called. The 300 members of management kept the plant operating during the strike with the supervisory and managerial personnel, but the pressures and demands of the effort exhausted management. The strike was also costly to the union, but successful in extracting from management certain contract terms it had long sought. Management felt that it was totally defeated, and the reactions of the union and its leadership bordered on arrogant pronouncements about what would happen "the next time."

Looking at the broader picture, management realized that the union-busting episode was only an extension of similar episodes that had occurred over a number of years. This observation led top management to ask itself, "Is it possible to reverse our relationship with the union and get out of this destructive win-lose course and into a problem-solving orientation?" Management considered approaching the union in an effort to investigate the issue of intergroup cooperation. When it did so the union curtly rejected the management proposal as "unworthy of consideration."

Sensing the situation as one of being locked into a system of prevailing norms, management decided to approach the study of the question from a behavioral science orientation.

Primary and Reference Group Participation

Of particular importance in understanding what was involved is an appreciation that attitudes toward the union extended far beyond those particular people who deal with the union on a daily basis. Therefore, management concluded that if norms of basic orientation were to be shifted, it was important that everyone working in the organization participate actively in studying such a possibility. The reason was that if only a few participated in the study and concluded that a change was both necessary and possible, the remaining members of the organization would probably see them as deviants who were violating the prevailing norms.

As a result, the entire management organization of 300 participated in a ten-hour discussion of the union–management relationship. This was done in seminars of 30, divided into leaderless discussion groups of 10 each. Ten such sessions were held on ten successive workdays, with three groups participating each day. The three top members of the company attended all seminars and each sat in one of the groups every day.

Identifying the Problem

A task paragraph focusing on the problem was prepared. After defining the problem, it asked: "What should the relationship between this management and this union be, and how can it be achieved?"

Using the task paragraph is an important step. By way of summary, a task paragraph concludes with open-ended statements that ask the questions "What is the real problem?" and "Can it be solved?" Every effort is made to write the task paragraph in as objective a way as possible. The purpose is to focus every participant's attention on the problem, not on the norms that are the background cause of the problem. The prevailing norm will emerge as the task paragraph is discussed.

In response to the task paragraph question, "What should the relationship between this management and this union be?" the initial reaction—part of the ventilation and catharsis period—was, "The union is led by thieves and crooks who want to destroy the company. It's win-lose with them all the way." This "them-ism" attitude had prevailed for years. Anyone who sought to make a positive approach to the union stood the risk of being labeled a Benedict Arnold and being isolated and rejected because he or she had deviated from a prevailing norm. The discussion served to clarify the extent to which past behaviors had been governed by this norm.

Norm-Shifting Discussions

Although there were variations from one group to another, the discussions were pretty much alike. The notion that "the union leadership is a bunch of thugs" was so deeply held and widely shared that the initial reaction was, "There is no possibility of change." This attitude was derived from a widespread norm that had come to be taken for granted by everyone who had suffered the frustrations of past efforts to deal with the union. Anyone who dared to take a more positive attitude would have risked being considered a heretic.

Much cathartic ventilation occurred. The result was that after the frustrations and anger had been discharged, there was nothing else to say. It was at this point that "new" thinking began to emerge on a "what if" basis.

As discussions continued, it became evident that management recognized it could not defeat the union and could not change its membership or leadership. Therefore, the only options were to continue the win-lose battle (more often than not coming out on the losing side) or try to change the relationship. In an effort to identify the underlying reasons for the existing relationship, many groups concluded that in fact management had become careless and had been spending more time trying to impress its holding company headquarters than running the plant in a more productive way.

In addition, it was acknowledged that many members of management were hostile merely because employees were members of an international union. This had come to the fore in meetings with union officers. Typical comments were, "We call a meeting with the union at 4:00 and terminate our discussions at 4:30. That way the union officers have to return to their workplace and spend ten minutes before they can leave, forcing them to exit in the middle of the traffic rush." Another was, "We take the longest allowable time in answering a grievance at each level in the grievance process." Still a third, "If bargaining is to begin at 10:00, we caucus until 10:30. The trouble is that the union people are beating us at our own game. When they see us coming, they caucus too, and we don't get started until 11:00."

At this point some people looked at a new question: "What would *we* have to do to get into a problem-solving relationship with the union?"

The antagonism felt toward the union had still not been resolved—someone was sure to say, "Give it a seat on the management committee," or "Cave in on the 30-hour week." Nonetheless, the idea began to emerge that the only possibility of changing the relationship was to treat the union and its officers with dignity and respect. The notion was advanced that union officers are elected officials who have status in legal terms. "It is not management's job to deprecate them as personalities and treat them as though they were evil. Management's only legitimate orientation is to work with them in a way that extends respect and that has the possibility of earning trust."

Consolidation of the New Norm

The seminar discussions were occasionally punctuated by general sessions in which the conclusions from the three groups were reported and contrasted to test whether a norm was emerging. In the course of these sessions, the inevitability of a converging norm became evident. By the seminar's end a positive conviction had been reached.

At the end of the ten-day period the word was passed through routine channels of the organization that every one of the groups had arrived at a closely similar conclusion. The conclusion was that it was important to establish a problem-solving relationship with the union. In order to do this, members of management were encouraged to treat the union and its officers with "dignity and respect." This conclusion reflected what had been emerging as a new norm, one that fit the attitudes and behavior that participants wanted for the organization. Now the job was to bring it into operational existence.

Implementation and Follow-up

The period of implementation and follow-up extended over a year and a half. It involved intensive efforts to help foremen and supervisors avoid being trigger-happy whenever they were approached with a grievance, to increase the speed with which grievances were answered, and to avoid deliberately provocative actions that might anger union officers.

From the standpoint of bargaining toward a new contract, management had gained enough open and respectful attention from the union leadership to propose a background review of the prevailing contract. The objective was to study the contract from the standpoint of future changes but without either side coming to the discussions with a prepared list of demands. As a result, both sides were able to present their rationale for certain paragraphs in the contract and to be open with each other about the shallowness or depth of the need to retain or delete certain paragraphs.

Eventually it became possible to reach agreement on entirely new paragraphs that increased management's flexibility while adding to the union's security. A new contract was prepared and signed, one that was far different from the previous one. Management had achieved a problem-solving relationship with the union that successfully replaced the win-lose relationship that had prevailed for years.

11
The Last Hour of Work

The problem of reduced productivity because of slacking off was brought up in the first chapter. We spoke of how employees in one plant more or less quit working an hour before the end of the workday and used that time for socializing. This chapter provides more background to help in understanding the problem.

Not only did supervisors in the plant spend the last hour of the day in their offices, but they could not predict with certainty the location of any employee during this hour. The reason was that employees had work-related justifications for being away from their primary area and in contact with employees in different sections. Thus, in this plant employees in any supervisory area might be supervised by that area's supervisor or by a supervisor from another area.

No one really knows how the practice of slacking off got started, but the tendency began to appear some years ago. When it first became evident, supervisors more or less ignored it. The presumption was that it was a temporary matter and that regular work practices would be resumed shortly. Yet the practice persisted and deepened into a chronic problem.

Diagnosing the Situation

In diagnosing the situation, management realized that the problem was out of control. Original policy had been replaced by a norm that legitimized slacking off as a way of slowing down.

Supervisors simultaneously backed off. Rather than exercise responsibility for achieving productivity, none of the supervisors were taking corrective action to rectify the problem among those for whom they were responsible. Each intuitively sensed that to take such an action would be unpopular and would probably bring criticism from both supervisory colleagues and from employees for trying to win points with management.

The diagnosis went beyond these considerations, because supervisors were hiding in their offices during the last hour of work in order to have an excuse for not doing something about the problem. They understood that if their boss never saw them in the area where social activities were taking place, no manager could complain that the supervisor "was right there and saw the problem and did nothing about it." This was particularly true if supervisors could justify their absence from the field of activity because they were "planning tomorrow's work."

The problem of slacking off was seen to represent a breakdown in supervisory effectiveness. Needed was the establishment of a new norm, accepted fully by all supervisors, so that each could feel support from the others in acting more responsible in solving the problem. With such a norm in place, any supervisor who failed to exercise responsibility for correcting the problem would become the deviant. The problem, therefore, was to help supervisors replace the "do nothing" norm with a norm of shared responsibility for maintaining productivity throughout the workday.

There are 20 supervisors who report to 4 managers. Over

the last several years, the managers have repeatedly discussed the problem among themselves. Different approaches to its resolution have been attempted one after another, all without measurable success.

One approach called for each manager to talk to his or her supervisors and explain the importance of having people apply their efforts during the last work hour. Each manager did talk to the supervisors and request each supervisor's help in resolving the difficulty. Nothing happened.

A second approach discussed by the managers was whether a symbolic firing of one or two supervisors might not signal to the rest that "we mean business." If this "message" could get through to the supervisors, it might settle the problem once and for all. This solution was not applied, however, because of fear that such firings would be demoralizing and would lead to even further reduction in productivity. Another possible approach was to employ two new supervisors who were not party to the past practices and who would therefore be freer to take the lead in bringing about needed changes.

Other possible solutions were discussed or tried, but none provided a satisfactory resolution of the problem. Finally, management made a determined effort to turn things around and instituted a series of meetings. The participants in this case were the 20 supervisors. They were in a position to resolve the problem and it was their responsibility to do so. Moreover, all of them needed to be involved in formulating and maintaining the new norm.

Identifying the Problem

The first action of the supervisors was to identify the causes of the problem in response to the following questions written on flip-chart paper: "What is the cause of the slacking-off problem? How can it be corrected?" Supervisors convened during the last hour of work to deal with these questions. Since the "do nothing" norm was shared by all the supervisors, they were gathered together in two leaderless groups of ten to discuss the problem.

It wasn't difficult for the discussion to get going. One supervisor said, "Attitudes toward work have changed. It's not like the old days. People expect to find more enjoyment nowadays and that's why they slow down." Another said, "The workers are older now. They feel their jobs are secure. They don't have to prove that they are hard workers. They know that they have jobs that will carry them to retirement if they wish to stay aboard." A third said, "The work they do isn't terribly interesting. Keeping your head concentrated on it seven hours is a pretty good achievement. Slowing down during the last hour is very understandable." A fourth said, "The real problem is the new generation. It has a more casual attitude than the last generation and it has infected everyone. What can we do about it? It's a hopeless situation."

Again, the "them-ism" problem is apparent, and we see the importance of having those who are involved in the problem think through and discuss whether their explanations have merit.

Each of the "them-ism" explanations was recorded on a flip chart for all to see. Finally, a different explanation was offered tentatively by one of the supervisors, who said, "When you come right down to it, the problem is that we're not supervising." Another quickly said, "Don't write that down. We don't want anybody to see that!" As the discussion continued, participants returned to the "we're not supervising" explanation of the problem. Someone else then asked, "If we are not supervising, why aren't we supervising? We are paid as supervisors." The discussion had now identified the "do nothing" norm. Each participant could verify it in terms of his or her own experiential reality.

The discussion became more involved as the supervisors

zeroed in on their own feelings. Someone said, "I know that none of you will do anything about the problem, and therefore if I do, all I'll get in return is kidding by the rest of you and criticism by employees. Why should I expose myself to that kind of hassle when I don't have to?" Others readily agreed. The general feeling emerged that none of the supervisors were confident of the readiness of other supervisors to come to grips with the problem. Now the cause had been identified.

Action Planning for Resolution

The next meeting dealt with exploring solutions to the problem. After some discussion, one supervisor made the following point: "I'm willing to take the initiative in solving the problem in my area, but only if the rest of you are willing to do likewise in your areas. I'm not going to do it if you're not going to." This comment introduced a very intense discussion of the extent to which supervisors would be willing to commit themselves to a new norm related to maintaining productivity throughout the workday. Some supervisors were reluctant to commit themselves to it for fear of a backlash.

As the meeting continued, the new norm began to emerge, but it was obvious that supervisors were unprepared to give their support to it until they had explored how it might be implemented. As the possibility of bringing this new norm into use was discussed, the notion was developed that implementation should take place in a stepwise way. Much discussion led to the formulation of the following action plan.

Week 1: Every supervisor meets with his or her employees to announce that supervisors across the organization have agreed that it is their responsibility to provide leadership in solving the slacking-off problem. Supervisors have uniformly committed themselves to doing so. During this week supervisors are asking employees to talk with one another and hopefully to give favorable consideration to helping supervisors bring the problem to a constructive solution.

Week 2: Supervisors begin implementing the new norm by becoming active in their work areas. When they see someone being sociable in an unproductive way, they ask the person to return to work but take no further action.

Week 3: Supervisors ask each person they see socializing in an unproductive way to get back to work, and they record the person's name if they know it, or ask the person his or her name if they don't know it. They report the person's name to the appropriate supervisor.

Week 4: If the problem persists, the supervisors interview those who are socializing in an unproductive way in order to make sure that the slackers understand the seriousness of the intent to solve the problem.

Week 5: If an employee persists in slacking off, a letter is placed in the file as a documentation preparatory to disciplinary action.

Week 6: If the behavior continues, the supervisor takes disciplinary action.

Development of this action plan proved to supervisors that a positive solution was feasible. By this time all supervisors had committed themselves to the new norm and to its implementation.

Implementing the Plan

During the first two weeks, the slacking-off phenomenon became the butt of considerable joking, not only among the hourly personnel but also between the workers and their supervisors. Remarks were made like, "Am I being sociable or is this a legitimate problem for us to be discussing?" However, it was evident that the announcement by the supervisors that they were committed to solving the problem was enough to clear the air and develop a widely shared positive attitude toward improving the situation. A few nudgings were necessary during the third week, but the problem had diminished to such a degree that no interviews were necessary, no letters of documentation were placed in the files, and no disciplinary action was needed.

The supervisors reconvened twice to review the situation— once at the end of the third week, and once at the end of the seventh week. They experienced great satisfaction that the problem had been solved and, beyond that, saw the importance of leading employees in a responsible way and supporting one another in the process of doing so.

The opposite of a backlash effect was observed in that morale seemed to have improved among supervisors and employees alike. One employee said, "To tell the truth, I always felt a little guilty toward the end of the day. I knew it wasn't quite right, but everyone else was doing it so I joined the gang. In fact, the time goes more rapidly when we stay busy."

This approach to the slacking-off problem is a good example of how norm shifting can be used to replace a "do nothing" norm that had been held in place by distrust. Any effort to solve the problem without replacing the "do nothing" norm was bound to have been unsuccessful simply because the true cause of the problem had not been diagnosed. Bringing the distrust that supervisors felt toward one another into focus provided the necessary insight and motivation to deal constructively with the real issue.

12
Designing
a Norm-Shifting Seminar

The last several chapters have provided specific illustrations of how unsatisfactory norms can be identified, evaluated, and rejected, and then replaced by stronger ones. Enough detail has been introduced to clarify the mechanics of this process. Now we return to these matters on a more systematic basis in order to explain how to go about norm shifting in particular situations.

Discussion Skills

It is evident that people who lack discussion skills simply do not have a very necessary tool for getting others to think through and talk about a problem. Yet discussion is a significant factor in aiding group members to become explicit about the norms that guide their behavior. A Grid seminar is an example of the kind of learning experience necessary for developing the skills essential for talking with others and getting people to work together in a constructive way. The Grid seminar is a five-day learning experience in which managers come face to face with issues of managing with and through people. Various ways of increasing the effectiveness of management are examined—such as confronting and resolving conflict, using critique to learn from experience, and establishing open and candid communication.

When an organization does not have anyone capable of leading such a discussion, a professional discussion leader is brought into the situation. Skills and talents vary from person to person, but a professional leader knows how to promote discussion by keeping the topic on track, asking questions of silent members to bring out their points of view, curbing overactive members in order to give others a chance to participate, helping resolve conflicting points of view by bringing them into bold relief, and so forth.[1] The alternative is for those who work together to acquire these needed discussion skills. But it is not usually necessary to bring a group leader in from the outside or even from another part of the organization because it is already routine for organization members to come together to talk about a problem, find an answer to it, and then separate. Much of this is done among colleagues, with no one person having more responsibility than the others for ensuring a positive outcome. The informality of colleague discussion groups enhances rather than inhibits discussion.

A recorder or spokesperson provides a sufficient degree of structure to keep track of conclusions and to exchange information between two or more groups that are engaged in studying the problem.

Leading the Norm-Shifting Effort

A rule of thumb is that at least two people should collaborate in designing and leading a norm-shifting effort. One of these is the line manager, whose ultimate responsibility it is to ensure successful problem solving where a problem exists. He or she is the person in charge, with the managerial responsibility for initiating discussions and leading subordinates in finding solutions to problems.

The other person often is the training and development professional, either an internal consultant or an outside expert who is brought into the organization for the purpose of helping with the problem at hand. The training and development professional, who works with the line manager, is successful when he or she provides technical support rather than active leadership. Support can be given by helping the line manager understand the strategy of norm shifting in preparing the task paragraph, in thinking through issues of group composition, in overcoming any excessive concern for the griping that may occur during a period of catharsis and ventilation, and in developing commitment to follow-up and ensuring that it occurs.

Seminar Length

Almost all the problems that are likely to arise from outmoded norms, norm erosion, and so on, can be grappled with in a seminar that lasts from 8 to 12 hours. The seminar can be conducted in one working day or, as described in Chapter 8, it may extend over two days to cover more complex subject matter, to cause minimum work disruption, or for some other reason.

The advantage of a two-day seminar—starting after lunch on day 1 and resuming on the morning of day 2—is that participants can ponder and review what they have learned on day 1 before returning the next day. This consolidation of thought and feeling can often add substantial benefit to the outcome.

The advantage of a continuous one-day seminar is that participants can get involved and stay involved without interruption. Many times this intensive concentration is necessary for achieving beneficial results. In these circumstances, the company frequently arranges for the noontime meal to be provided. The benefit is that participants have the opportunity to relax during a meal together, and the camaraderie contributes to cohesion.

Seminar Composition

The seminar should include all those who can contribute to the solution of the problem or who are part of the problem. When you are in doubt, it's best to err on the side of broad attendance. Otherwise, you may exclude members of a reference group or even members of the primary group who play a significant role in regulating behavior. Given that broad generalization, the specific composition of the seminar can be approached in four ways.

One approach is to take a horizontal slice of the organization. A horizontal slice means that those who attend are all from the same level. For example, in the slacking-off case discussed earlier, the 20 supervisors had the problem, and only they, from a practical point of view, could solve it. Attendance at the seminar by others not directly responsible for supervision would have contributed nothing.

A second possibility is a diagonal slice. A diagonal slice means that people of varying ranks and departmental memberships come together to deal with a problem, each from his or her own perspective. Thus the head of the engineering department may be in a seminar group with a section head from the maintenance department and a front-line supervisor from an operating segment. In addition to line personnel, staff members may also attend. The diagonal slice is exemplified in Chapter 10, in the discussion of union–management relations.

The rationale for the diagonal slice is that both primary and reference groups share the basic norm that is under scrutiny. Only by having *all* concerned people think through and commit themselves is it possible for any one person to avoid being seen as a deviant for advocating a shift in behavior away from prevailing norms. An additional advantage to the diagonal slice is that many more perspectives can be brought to bear on the topic at hand.

Some problems that exist between two or more levels do not involve the total diagonal slice of an organization. Thus a third possibility is a truncated diagonal slice. The safety problem discussed in Chapter 9 provided an example: seminar attendees were supervisors and wage and salaried personnel. Only those people were directly involved in the safety problem; therefore, it was they who needed to collaborate on its solution.

A fourth possibility is the vertical slice. The vertical group consists of at least two levels—the boss and those subordinates who report to him or her—and sometimes more than two levels. The vertical slice involves people of different ranks in the same reporting chain. Issues related to norms at the lower levels of the vertical slice often cannot be dealt with directly until the power and authority issues at higher levels have been resolved.

Group Composition Within the Seminar

The composition of groups within a seminar ordinarily replicates the composition of the seminar itself. If a seminar is based on a diagonal slice, the groups themselves should have the character of a diagonal slice.

Occasionally someone specifically asks, "Who should be grouped with whom?" Many corporate groups are put together on the "mastermind" premise: "I know which people would have the most stimulating discussion if they were placed together." Our experience is that this kind of masterminding is more often wrong than right. In any event, it is unnecessary. A mechanical assembling of people that respects the slice character of the seminar is much more satisfactory.

Implementation and Follow-up

Implementation and follow-up are significant to success. Often what might otherwise result in dramatic change fails to do so because of the widespread notion that a problem is "solved" once a solution has been identified. It is important to arrange for ongoing review and analysis as well as consolidation of the new behavior as part of the total effort to ensure that fadeout or backing off does not occur.

NOTES

1. The use of a professional discussion leader to promote participation, which is characteristic of many QWL efforts to increase productivity, suffers the limitation of supplementing inadequate interaction skills of organization members rather than training people directly. Under these circumstances, when the professional leaves and participants try on their own to take the next steps, the program falters because they lack the skills for doing so. This problem is recognized from within the QWL movement itself. See T. Chase, "Another Varied, Rich Ecology of Work Conference," *OD Practitioner*, October 1980, *12*(3): 10. The reference quotes T. Mills, who among others is a leader in the QWL movement and is president of the American Center of Quality of Work Life. See also S. P. Rubinstein, "QWL and the Technical Societies," *Training and Development Journal*, August 1980, *34*(8): 76–81.

This same limitation is inherent in catalytic or facilitative team building as a way of bringing about changes in norms. The use of the facilitator or catalyst in team building is described in E. Schein, *Process Consultation: Its Role in Organization Development*. Reading, Mass.: Addison-Wesley, 1969.

13
Releasing Creativity
Within Groups

A great many problems of industrial life can be analyzed in terms of the basic premises that have been formulated in earlier chapters:

1. Whenever several people discuss a topic for which the answer is not self-evident, they tend to influence one another and their thinking converges into norms.

2. Once a norm is established, conformity pressures arise, and the nonconformist is subject to these pressures.

3. A person who persists in deviating from the norm risks being isolated and rejected.

4. The greater the cohesion among members, the greater the readiness of people to converge; the greater the support of the norms, once established; and the greater the pressure to conform.

5. Everyone feels stress and strain when seeking to maintain independence in the face of conformity pressures, and many yield their convictions with or without being aware of doing so.

6. Competition with another group or threat of defeat may significantly strengthen pressure toward conformity.

We can now examine a few additional premises and try to understand their far-reaching implications for independent thinking and creativity.

"Groupthink"

Groupthink is a word that describes what happens when a discussion results in convergence on invalid conclusions. This may occur in a number of ways. The problem itself may be incorrectly identified and the quality of inquiry of group discussion may not be good enough to challenge it. Or options for solving the problem may not be fully identified and, again, the character of discussion may be too weak to probe the pros and cons of each option sharply. When thinking is shallow, convergence may appear prematurely and may not be subject to challenge.

It is said that this description precisely fits what happened when President John F. Kennedy and his key advisers converged on a decision resulting in the Bay of Pigs fiasco.[1] The same type of convergence led the Ford Motor Company to the decision to produce the Edsel, which became a financial disaster for the company.[2]

Any group that engages in discussion, from the board of directors on down to operating levels, may potentially victimize itself by the groupthink process. Some of the dynamics responsible for groupthink include the following.

1. Charismatic leadership. A charismatic leader whose thinking is characterized by flair and broad leaps from diagnosis to conclusion can gain unthinking acceptance of proposals. People with charm literally draw others to them. Convergence forms rapidly, usually on whatever position the charismatic leader is promoting.

2. Cohesion. When the members of a group feel cohesive—drawn to the group as an entity from which they derive prestige and drawn to other members because they like them—it is more difficult for analytical thinking to occur. As a result, members are more easily persuaded to accept a point of convergence even though it may be unsound by objective criteria.

3. Crisis. Convergence is likely to occur around a false position when decisions need to be reached quickly and time for discussion is minimal.

4. Importance and difficulty. When an important and complex problem is at hand, finding the solution may be very difficult, and the consequences of that solution may be serious. These circumstances arouse great insecurities among the people who must deal with the problem. Such people become more susceptible to influence from others, which leads to the increased possibility of convergence around a position that is unsound.

Many students of management are aware of the existence of groupthink and try to avoid it by reducing group discussion to a minimum. This "solution" to a groupthink problem is based on a faulty understanding of the dynamics behind it. It is not that groupthink is "caused" by the involvement of many people in thinking together; rather it is caused by the failure of group members to grapple with convergence and conformity pressures.

The conclusion that, other things being equal, unilateral decision making is preferable to group discussion is unjustified. The deeper issue is that many problems are of a character that makes discussions necessary, if not inevitable; and if group members are unaware of the operation of convergence and conformity pressures, they are more likely to be victimized by them.

Creativity

Creativity can be described as the process of identifying a problem that was previously unrecognized or identifying a solution to a problem that is not within the prior experience of any of those involved. We can see that creativity is at the opposite end of the spectrum from conformity or groupthink.

Research on creativity has centered on individual traits of personality that make one person an innovator and another a traditionalist. There is some value in this approach, but there is even greater value in knowing that our thinking processes are basically social in character. This can be supported in many ways, not the least of which is that much thinking takes place in language, and language is a social tool. People are social creatures. Even when they are completely "alone," as when reading a book, they are communicating with the author. Possibly the reader's own thinking is converging with the author's point of view.

Let's take a very personal look to see how our thinking is influenced. If you, the reader, were to propound these ideas about the social character of creative thinking, you might encounter repudiation. If in anticipation of such rejection you were to moderate your advocacy, you would be yielding to conformity pressure even before it was exerted.

Convergence, conformity pressures, and the maintenance of independence are all phenomena that influence private thinking. Therefore, individual creativity can be reduced even when there is no active attempt to influence a person's thinking.

Let's examine these phenomena from the point of view of their effect on creative thinking. We already know something about them from previous discussion.

Convergence

People who are interacting tend to converge toward a single position, which in turn becomes the norm of thought, attitude, and feeling. The natural motivation to converge is unrelated to group pressure. It is a "fact" of social existence that cooperation and coordination literally require people who are interacting to develop norms, implicit or otherwise.

We know intuitively that it is in our best interests to work with and among, even in behalf of, the social group to which we belong. However important and useful this fact may be, it is inimical to creativity.

Conformity Pressures

The pressure to conform produces a closed-minded outlook and imposes sanctions on those who do not adhere to the majority position. Innovative thinking leads people to express novel ideas or to take unpopular positions that they themselves may only partially understand and that others may not understand at all. The rapidity with which conformity pressures can crush original ideas and prevent them from gaining the attention they merit can now be appreciated. We can see clearly what a negative effect they have and how they inhibit creative thinking, since thinking differently is one basis for rejection.

Maintenance of Independence

We saw in Chapter 6 how difficult it is to retain independence, even when the issue is one of visual perception and objectivity and physical reality is readily available for inspection. In spite of this, when conformity pressures are uniform in a false direction, as many as one-third of a typical population yields to the pressures exercised upon it. People deny physical reality rather than risk rejection for expressing "different" perceptions.

We see now that the social processes of convergence and resultant conformity pressures, which make cooperation and coordination possible, can also have two undesirable results. One of these is groupthink; the other is the stifling of creativity. Experts who have investigated the field of creativity have come to recognize these matters. They offer suggestions for encouraging creativity by adopting and implementing unique discussion procedures.

"Walling Off" Conformity

There are two approaches to "walling off" the conformity pressures that constrict divergent thinking. One of these is brainstorming,[3] a popular procedure that imposes the norm of no evaluation. In this approach participants are asked to free-associate and come up with new ideas, no matter how offbeat they may sound. People are encouraged to produce ideas whether they make sense or not. They are encouraged to withhold judgment. The ideas produced in an uncritical, spontaneous, intuitive way become a pool of possibilities.

After the brainstorming session, judgment is exercised in evaluating the ideas produced. Now each idea is subject to the rigorous steps of analysis characteristic of logical, precise thinking. The group that evaluates the "original" ideas may be composed of different people to free those who produce ideas from the evaluative pressures of colleagues.

A related approach is a technique for creating conditions under which "free" thinking can occur before judgment is exercised. Dual leadership is given to a group that is seeking a creative solution to a problem.[4] One leader is responsible for the social and emotional climate of the discussion—particularly during the phase when ideas are being generated. That person must restrain participants from making evaluations at this time. The other leader is the person who is in need of a creative solution, the "task" leader. The task leader does not exercise judgment while ideas are being produced; he or she focuses the discussion after idea production has been completed, when innovative possibilities are being evaluated for their usefulness and practicality.

Both of these approaches are "mechanical" ways to solve the problems of convergence and conformity pressure. They go around the issue rather than dealing with it directly. Extensive research indicates that they do not solve the problem of how to promote creative thought. In the light of this contrary evidence, it is surprising that the approaches retain some degree of popularity.[5]

Another approach recognizes that a person, whether in a group or alone, may exercise self-induced convergence effects and conformity pressures. It sets out rules of thinking that are calculated to aid a person or a group to view a problem from altered perspectives and in this way increase the likelihood of finding creative solutions. Three rules govern this creativity-inducing process:[6]

1. Focus on intermediate possibilities that may themselves be wrong or impossible but may be used as a steppingstone to a new idea that is right.
2. Create a juxtaposition of random ideas to stimulate a new way of viewing the problem.
3. Bypass or set aside ideas that appear to "solve" a problem until alternative ways of looking at a situation can be generated.

These three rules seek to prevent the premature exercise of judgment by an individual whose thoughts stem from personal experience or by a group that stifles departure from the status quo by exerting pressure to conform.

Creativity and Social Dynamics Skills

The circumstances that are most conducive to creative thinking are those in which the people who have responsibility for the work understand in a first-hand way the convergence phenomenon and conformity pressures and how they operate; how easy it is to yield and how difficult it is to retain independence. When the dynamics of these creativity-reducing phenomena are understood and people can therefore consciously work to nullify their effects, norms that support creativity can emerge. This is the result of training.

Experts on creativity have made numerous efforts to reduce convergence and conformity effects in order to create conditions under which innovations can more easily occur. As we have seen, group props to creativity include suspending judgment while "free" thinking takes place and introducing two leaders, one to stimulate creativity and the other to act as the operational leader once innovations have appeared. Another approach is based on "rules" that reduce convergence or conformity effects.

The more genuine solution, of course, is for group members to become fully aware of—and to constrain—those aspects of their own behavior that might promote convergence and conformity at the expense of valid thinking and to help others do the same. Thus the best approach to stimulating creativity in groups is to have members acquire discussion skills that make it possible for them to retain independence, even in the face of conformity pressures. This is particularly true when the exercise of independence is critical to the complete and objective examination of the problem, the development of alternatives, and the full exploration of the pros and cons of each.

Perhaps the best available model for bringing creative thinking to bear on resolving problems is the scientific model of the experiment. In an experiment preexisting thinking and attitudes are deliberately set aside in order to test a proposition or hypothesis. The rigorousness of thought and the thoroughness of preparation necessary for designing and conducting an experiment often provide the right conditions for finding unique, innovative, and creative solutions. The model permits people to look at alternatives without feeling any pressure to conform to preexisting positions, because it is an "experiment," or trial. That is, people are not being asked to change their minds initially, only to open them to other alternatives.

The evidence that surfaces in an experiment enables people to see the potentialities for solving the problem from different points of view. Finally, when a solution is demonstrated through the procedures of experimental verification, convictions formerly based on opinions or subjective distortions can be replaced by convictions rooted in objectivity.

NOTES

1. See I. L. Janis. *Victims of Groupthink*. Boston: Houghton Mifflin, 1972. Janis, in a series of historical analyses, examined four major U.S. foreign policy decisions that were considered examples of groupthink. These include the Bay of Pigs invasion, crossing the thirty-eighth parallel in the Korean War, failure to be prepared for Pearl Habor, and escalation of the Vietnam War. Janis makes the point that the decision to act or not to act was made by a highly cohesive group that was relatively isolated. In the effort to maintain an atmosphere of congeniality, group members failed to make critical evaluations of the available information and to maintain a questioning point of view. Thus they failed to make the best possible decision. Janis summarizes the conditions likely to produce groupthink:
   —Members feel invulnerable and optimistic about their success and therefore take risks.
   —Members make an effort to discount warnings that challenge their positive evaluation of the group's effectiveness.
   —Members hold an unquestioned belief in the group's inherent morality—that is, they have a strong allegiance to norms.
   —Members holds stereotypical views of the outgroup as being less effective than they are.
   —Pressures are brought to bear to bring a member who disagrees back into line.
   —Members use self-censorship to get rid of deviant thoughts or doubts.
   —Members hold an illusion of unanimity among themselves that matches the majority but not necessarily the consensus point of view.
   —"Mind guards," or members who protect the group from information that might shatter their complacency, emerge (pp. 197–198).
All these criteria seem to have been present in the failure of the top management of General Motors to develop a market for a small fuel-efficient car during the period 1965–1980, when foreign carmakers were hewing out more than 25 percent market share in the United States. See J. P. Wright, *On a Clear Day You Can See General Motors*. New York: Avon Books, 1979.

2. J. Brooks, "The Fate of the Edsel," *Business Ventures*. New York: Weybright and Talley, 1969. (Originally appeared in *The New Yorker*.)

3. Alex Osborne. *Wake Up Your Mind: 101 Ways to Develop Creativeness.* New York: Scribners, 1952.

4. In his approach to creativity, W. J. Gordon has paid particular attention to the social processes that are likely to inhibit the spontaneous production of innovative ideas. See. W. J. Gordon, *Synectics: The Development of Creative Capacity.* New York: Macmillan, 1968.

5. W. K. Graham, "Acceptance of Ideas Generated Through Individual and Group Brainstorming." *Journal of Social Psychology,* 1977, *101:* 231–234. See also H. Lamm and G. Trommsdorf, "Group Versus Individual Performance on Tasks Requiring Ideational Proficiency (Brainstorming): A Review," *European Journal of Social Psychology,* 1973, *3*(4): 361–388.

6. E. de Bono, *New Think: The Use of Lateral Thinking in the Generation of New Ideas.* New York: Basic Books, 1968. De Bono gives the following example of how an intermediate impossible solution may suggest a creative approach to the problem.

Many areas in one production location tended to be dirty. Management frequently complained about inadequate cleaning, but the cleanup crew insisted that the work it did was adequate. An intermediate impossible statement about this dilemma is, "The best way to clean the workplace is to dirty it more." This seems absurd, but by going in the opposite direction to solve the problem, management came up with a steppingstone to an idea that did make sense. In this case the supervisors periodically scattered tiny pieces of colored paper in the aisles, making a record of the date on which certain colors were used. In this way the efficiency of the cleaning crew could be determined by the length of time the paper remained on the floor.

14
Conclusion

Behavioral science theory and research are invaluable sources of insight on human problems of effectiveness in business, industry, health delivery, education, and other major institutions of society. Their value derives from the fact that they make us see problems in a different light from the one in which we normally perceive them, thereby enabling us to solve these problems rather than just live with them. Without principles to inform our judgment, we are likely to interpret what we see on the basis of personal experience, commonsense notions, attitudes formed by the norms of our membership groups, or precedents rooted in the history of the organization.

A Family of Ideas

The behavioral science research which leads to generalizations about the impact of convergence, conformity, cohesion, yielding, independence, and groupthink on a person's thoughts and actions is a case in point. Because these few basic concepts are interrelated, they constitute a very pow-

118

erful family of ideas to help us understand the social dynamics of productivity and creativity. It has been possible to use these ideas along the way to clarify many important phenomena that often appear to be inaccessible and to defy interpretation.

For example, we learned how the maintenance of independence can be strengthened or reduced and how important an ally is in helping someone maintain independence when he or she has a different point of view from that being expressed in the group. This basic finding, in turn, led us to an appreciation of why so many important leaders are supported by a confidant, a person to whom they can turn automatically for constructive testing out of their point of view.

Apart from this, we saw that the same underlying theory and research had application to an entirely different phenomenon. We were able to use these concepts to demonstrate the consolidation of leadership that takes place when a group has been successful. We could also demonstrate the risks of the group rigidifying and perpetuating its conduct on the basis of norms that soon became outmoded. By comparison, the norms of conduct in place when a group is led to defeat are quickly rejected and replaced by new norms. The leadership that had been responsible for the imposition of the old norms is also rejected.

These concepts also help us understand some of the most significant developments among nations in this century. Great Britain and the United States, as victorious groups in World War II, retained the leaders who had brought victory and the norms of conduct that had been characteristic of the military period. The predictable result was that these countries became fat, happy, and complacent and have continued to find it difficult to break away from the outmoded norms that are barriers to progress. By the same token, the defeated groups in World War II, Germany and Japan, rejected the norms that led to their defeat and turned from the leaders who had been responsible for them. As a result of this "lean and hungry" approach to the future, these countries have managed to be far more innovative and to penetrate world markets in a far more aggressive way than the winners.

If we can gain real understanding of this relatively small constellation of behavioral science concepts through experimentation and research, we have a very powerful tool to help us understand and manage institutional phenomena that are otherwise essentially out of control. We are accustomed to seeing problems and problem solving in the context of individuals. We are far less accustomed to looking at someone from the standpoint of his or her group membership commitments. Yet to see the problems of people as actually centered in memberships but still try to deal with them on a person-to-person basis is unlikely to have a constructive outcome.

This was illustrated, for example, in the slacking-off problem. Initial efforts to get supervisors to talk with their employees about being productive during the last hour of work did not meet with positive action. The supervisors intuitively sensed the pressures they would face if they started acting as eager beavers to bring the problem under control. When the issue was seen as a group problem shared by all supervisors, it was not difficult to grapple with it and to design a constructive program for bringing about a resolution.

Other examples—on accident-proneness and union–management relations—demonstrated a similar phenomenon. In each of the cases, what was initially seen as a problem of "individuals" turned out in fact to be caused by membership commitments. Therefore, the key is in diagnosing and solving *group* problems. In this way, people can be released from the conformity pressures that hold unproductive behaviors in place.

Many problems are not related to norms, at least not in a primary sense. Rather, they are the consequence of bad or inappropriate use of power and authority. As long as people are antagonistic toward the authority being exercised on them, or have ceased being involved to the point of becoming apathetic, any effort to change norms will not be effective. Problems that are centered on the faulty use of power and authority can be solved only when managers learn better ways to exercise that power and authority, ways that promote involvement and active participation rather than indifference.

Other problems prevail because of the absence of a sense of purpose—employees may literally lack a goal orientation. If employees have no sense of direction, no objectives to be committed to, any effort to solve the problem as a norms issue is destined to failure. The only solution is to develop goals and objectives. The same can be said of morale and cohesion. If morale has dropped to such a low level that people have ceased caring and are indifferent to how problems are solved, no attempt to change norms will be effective. When people no longer feel committed to the organization, the only way to turn things around is to deal directly with the cause. Why have people stopped feeling involved in the jobs that constitute their employment? Only when this question is answered and steps taken to restore morale and cohesion is there any significant likelihood that progress can be made.

Who "Owns" the Problem?

With these precautions in mind, we can move to solve a great variety of problems by our understanding that they are the result of outmoded norms or norms that have eroded to such a low level that people act unrealistically from the standpoint of the organization's needs for achievement.

If the use of behavioral science research and theory on convergence, conformity pressures, cohesion, and the maintenance of independence is to be effective, the line manager, as a behavioral science practitioner, must avoid two possible misdefinitions of the problem. The first trap is seeing individuals as the source of the problem. If a manager says, in effect, that a person is unproductive because it's characteristic of him or her, then a false solution may be to remove that person and hire another. If the level of productivity in fact is anchored in group norms of low output, then the next person will be as likely to be influenced by these norms as the person who was replaced. Thus low output persists. The second trap is presuming the group to be the problem. Viewing the group as a collection of individuals may also blind the manager to the norms that hold individual attitudes and values in place. To avoid these two traps, the manager must ask: "Who are the several people who have this problem in common? Who are the ones who would have to reach agreement if all were to implement a single solution?"

By starting with the problem and identifying those who "own" it, the manager can see what has previously been invisible—namely, that the problem belongs not to one person but rather to several people by virtue of their group membership and that the problem is brought about by convergence, group pressures to conform, and the difficulty of separating the individual from the membership group as a target of change.

The difficulty is that we have not trained ourselves to "see" convergence. As a matter of course, we do not "see" norms; we do not "see" group pressures. And when we "see" someone stoutly defending an independent position, we are far more likely to view that person as a renegade than as a creative thinker.

Behavioral science research and theory on norms offer valuable insights for operational problem solving. When understood and implemented in a sound way, they can increase productivity and release creativity in any and every organizational setting, from business and government to schools and hospitals.

Index

academic tenure, 48
accidents, analyzing, 81–82
advancement, cohesion as
   factor in, 37–38
Allen, V.L., 62n
allies
   conformity and, 62n
   importance of, 119
   independence affected by,
      56–57, 62n
alternatives, examination of, 57
American Center of Quality of
   Work Life, 107n
American Medical Association,
   71
The American Soldier, Vol. 1,
   *Adjustments During Army
   Life* (Stoffer et al.), 16n
anonymity, independence
   fostered by, 56
antagonism, *see* competition
antagonists, 59–60

Archives of Psychology, Sherif
   study described in, 33n
Asch, S.E., 33n
Aspects of Educational Change
   (Morrish), 62n
attitudes
   convergence of, *see*
      convergence
   distribution of, 42n
   norms vs., 18, 23–24
   personal nature of, 14, 17, 23
   toward productivity, 13–15
authority, faulty use of, 121
autokinetic effect, 25–26
automobile industry, 45, 67–68

Bay of Pigs incident, 109, 116n
behavior
   attitudes vs., 14
   changing, 73–74
   convergence and, 28
   norms and, 20–22

125

behavioral science
  insights offered by, 118–123
  norms explained by, 69
  philosophy of, 14
Behaviorism (Watson), 15n
The Behavior of Organisms
  (Skinner), 15n
Bennington College, 71, 80n
Berscheid, E., 61n
Beyond Freedom and Dignity
  (Skinner), 16n
blame in norm-shifting process,
  79, 83–84, 90–91, 98
brainstorming, 113
Byrne, D., 41n

catalytic team building, 107n
catharsis in norm-shifting
  process, 79, 84–85, 90
change, resistance to, 72–74
charismatic leadership, dangers
  of, 109
Churchill, Winston, 67
cohesion
  acceptance vs. rejection in,
    46–47
  advancement and, 37–38
  competition as factor in, 65
  convergence and, 37
  groupthink resulting from,
    109–110
  norms and, 37
  in organizational life, 37–39
  phenomenon of, 35–36
  productivity and, 39–40
  promoting, 121
  success as factor in, 65
  in World War II, 66
commands, uselessness of, 73
competence, independence
  resulting from, 56, 61n

competition
  conformity caused by, 108
  dynamics of, 66–68
  among groups, 64–66
complacency, 67, 119
compliance, *see* conformity
conclusions, invalid, 109
Conditioned Reflexes (Pavlov),
  15n
confidant, independence
  fostered by, 58–59, 119
conflict, *see* competition
*Conflict, Decision, and
  Dissonance* (Festinger), 33n
conformity
  in academic institutions, 48
  awareness of, 115
  brainstorming to prevent,
    113
  in business, 47–48
  competition as factor in, 108
  creativity vs., 110–112
  dangers of, 44–45
  dynamics of, 45–48
  enforcement of, 47
  free thinking to prevent,
    113–114
  in government, 48
  human need for, 54
  "lip service," 49, 50–51n
  operation of, 43–45
  outward, 49
  pressure for, 46, 108
  pressures of, 49
  self-induced, 114
  studies on, 38–39
  susceptibility to, 38–39
  understanding, 114–115
  "walling off," 113
Conformity (Kiesler), 51n
consultants, 58

convergence
  awareness of, 115
  cohesion and, 37
  competition and, 65
  complexity as factor in, 110
  evidence of, 32–33
  experiments in, 25–27
  inhibiting, 113
  on invalid conclusions, 109
  invisibility of, 30, 32–33
  in organizational life, 28–30
  persistence of, 26–28
  phenomenon of, 26
  premature, 109
  productivity and, 39–40
  rejection as factor in, 48
  self-induced, 114
  social reality and, 30–33
  social roots of, 111–112
  thought processes and,
    111–112
  understanding of, 114–115
cooperation, norms as factor in,
  49, 54–55
creativity
  altered perspectives in, 114
  conditions for, 115
  encouraging, 114
  experimentation in
    promoting, 115–116
  social nature of, 110–111
  social processes inhibiting,
    117*n*
  understanding social
    dynamics of, 119
crisis, groupthink and, 110
customs, 20
  see also norm(s)

Darley, J.M., 61*n*
Darwin, Charles, 55

De Bono, E., 117*n*
decision making, unilateral vs.
  group, 110
decrees, ineffectiveness of, 73
defeat, characteristics of,
  65–67, 119–120
deviants
  group members as, 72
  isolation of, 44, 46, 72
  pressure applied to, 44, 46,
    55, 72
  rejection of, 44, 46–48, 55, 72
  structural, 59–60
  studies on, 62*n*
  see also independence;
    innovators
devil's advocate, 57
discussion(s)
  climate of, 113
  convergence in, 108
  groupthink resulting from,
    109–110
  informal, 103
  leadership in, 103, 107*n*, 113
  minimizing, 110
  skills required for, 102–103,
    115
  see also seminars
Dittes, J.E., 38
Duval, S., 61*n*

Eisenhower, Dwight D., 67
empirical reality, 31
equipment and productivity, 7
enthusiasm in motivation, 4–5
experiential reality, norms and,
  31–32
experimentation, creativity
  encouraged by, 115–116

facilitative team building, 107*n*
fear as motivation, 4

Festinger, L., 33n
firing, symbolic, 97
follow-up to norm shifting, 79,
   93–94, 107
Ford Motor Company, 109
free-association, 113
"free" thinking, conditions for,
   113

General Motors Corporation,
   45, 116n
Germany, 66–67, 120
goals, development of, 121
Gordon, W.J., 116n
Great Britain, 66–67, 119
Grid seminars, 102–103
group pressure
   anticipated, 48–49
   competition and, 65
   conformity resulting from,
      48–50, 112
   dangers of, 112
   patterns of, 44, 46–48, 72,
      108
   resisting, 52–60
   susceptibility to, 56
groups
   characteristics of, 17–20
   competition among, 64–66
   composition of, in norm-
      shift-in seminars, 105–107
   external influences on, 63
   formation of, 34–35
   individuals vs., 18
   infighting in, 65
   interaction in, 60
   interrelationship among,
      63–64
   loyalty to, 65
   membership in, 70–72
   norms in, see norm(s)

pressure in, see group
   pressure
primary, 70
reference, 70
religion as factor in, 37
socioeconomic factor in, 37
supervisors constituting, 8
technical-practical
   distinction in, 37
groupthink, 109–110
   examples of, 116n

habits, 19
   see also norm(s)
Human Relations
   Gerard study described in,
      51n
   Schachter study described in,
      50–51n

independence
   as admirable quality, 57
   allies as factor in, 56–57
   anonymity as factor in, 56
   competence and, 56
   confidant as factor in, 58–59
   delusion of, 28
   devil's advocate and, 57
   encouraging, 60
   experiments in, 53–54
   group dynamics and, 60
   innovation as result of, 55
   maintaining, 52–60, 108, 119
   rejection of, 55
   self-esteem and, 56
   of structural deviants, 59–60
   understanding, 114
   see also deviants
individuals vs. groups, 18
infighting in groups, 65
influence, see convergence

informal systems, 20
  see also norm(s)
innovation
  conformity as threat to,
    44–45, 112
  encouraging, 114–116
  independence as factor in, 55
  norms as barrier to, 21
  see also creativity
innovators, 62*n*, 112
instruction, ineffectiveness of, 97
intergroup conflict, 64–67
involvement, lack of, 121
Italy, 66–67

Jackson, J.M., 38
Janis, I.L., 116*n*
Japan, 66–67, 120
job redesign, 5
*Journal of Abnormal and Social
    Psychology*, Schachter
    study described in, 50*n*
*Journal of Experimental Social
    Psychology*
  Allen and Levine study
    described in, 62*n*
  Darley, Moriarity and
    Berscheid experiment
    described in, 61*n*
  Duval study described in, 61*n*

Kelley, H.H., 38
Kennedy, John F., 109
Kiesler, C.A., 51*n*

Lage, E., 62*n*
leadership
  capacity for, 57–58
  charismatic, 109
  consolidation of, 66–67
  in norm-shifting process, 76,
    103–104

Levine, J.M., 62*n*
line managers
  guidelines for, 122
  in norm-shifting process,
    103–104
"lip service" conformity, 49,
  50–51*n*
loyalty, competition and, 65

MacArthur, Douglas, 66
Malcolm X, 36
management-by-objectives
  (MBO), 5–6
Managerial Grid, 80*n*
managers, line, *see* line managers
Marshall, George, 66
Marshall Plan, 67
Marx, Karl, 55
MBO (management-by-
  objectives), 5–6
Mills, T., 107*n*
morale, restoring, 121
Moriarity, T., 61*n*
Morrish, Ivan, 21*n*
Moscovici, S., 62*n*
motivation
  fear as, 4
  job redesign as, 5
  MBO and, 5–6
  participation and, 5–7
  productivity and, 4–5
  quality circles (QC) and, 6–7
  quality of work life (QWL)
    and, 6
  rah-rah, 4–5

nonconformity, *see* deviants;
  independence
norm(s)
  accommodation to, 74
  attitudes vs., 18, 23–24

norm(s) *(cont.)*
behavioral analysis of, 69
behavior and, 20–22
cohesion and, 37
conformity to, *see* conformity
context of, 24
convergence in formation of, 26–28
corporate objectives served by, 75
defined, 17, 20
deviation from, *see* deviants; independence
emergence of new, 92–93, 99
explanations offered for, 79
external influences on, 67
formation of, 24–26
group membership and, 69–72
identifying, 75, 77
implementation of new, 93–94
organizational, 71–72
outmoded, 21, 44–45, 55, 67, 119
in primary groups, 70, 72
problems underlying, 77–78
productivity and, 21–22
in professional societies, 71
reality and, 31–32
in reference groups, 70–72
rejection, private, of, 49, 51*n*
resistance of, to authority, 73
shared, 40
shifting of, *see* norm shifting
strength of, 72–74
supervisory, 8–10
task paragraph in study of, 77–78
in union-management relationships, 90–91

norm shifting
blame in, 79, 83–84, 90–91, 98
catharsis in, 79, 84–85, 90
commitment to, 86–87
context of, 79–80
defeat as impetus for, 65–67, 119–120
discussion process in, 82–86
discussion skills in, 102–103
explicit agreements accompanying, 79, 92–93
follow-up to, 79, 93–94, 100–101
implementation of, 93–94, 99–101
leadership in, 76, 103–104
objective data as factor in, 78–79, 83–85
participation in, 75–76
professional assistance in, 104
responsibility for, 103–104
in safety management, 82–86
seminars in, *see* seminars
in slacking-off behavior, 95–101
strategy for, 75–80
support for, 75
team building in, 107*n*
unified approach to, 99
in union-management relationship, 88–94

objectives, development of, 121
objectivity, experiments to establish, 116
organizations
attitudes toward, 38
cohesion in, 37–39
convergence in, 28–30

participation
as motivation, 5–7

in norm shifting process,
  75–80
problems of, 6–7
Pavlov, I.P., 14, 15n
pay, productivity and, 2
persuasion, productivity and,
  49
physical reality, 31
piece rate system, 2
policies, 19–20
  see also norm(s)
*The Polish Peasant in Europe
  and America* (Thomas), 16n
power, faulty use of, 121
precedents, 19
  see also norm(s)
primary groups, 70
productivity
  attitudes toward, 13–15
  backlash in, 49–50
  behavior vs. attitudes in,
    14–15
  cohesion and, 39–40
  conformity as threat to,
    49–50
  convergence and, 39–40
  demoralization affecting, 97
  equipment and, 7
  importance of, 1
  job redesign and, 5
  MBO and, 5–6
  motivation in, 4–5
  norms regulating, 21–22, 40
  participation and, 5–7
  pay and, 2
  persuasion and, 49
  quality circles (QC) and, 6–7
  quality of work life (QWL)
    and, 6–7
  rewards for, 49
  scientific management and, 2

selection and, 3
shared attitudes toward, 40
social dynamics of, 119
sociotechnical systems and, 7
supervision and, 3–4, 8–10
training and, 3
professional societies, 71
Psychological Monographs, Asch
  study described in, 33n
psychological testing, 3
*The Psychology of Industrial
  Conflict* (Stagner), 16n
The Psychology of Social Norms
  (Sherif), 16n
purpose, lack of, 121

QC, *see* quality circles
quality circles (QC), 6–7
  weaknesses of, 76
quality of work life (QWL), 6
  professional discussion leader
    in, 107n
  weaknesses of, 76
QWL, *see* quality of work life

rah-rah motivation, 4–5
reality
  convergence and, 30–34
  physical vs. social, 31
reference groups, 70
regulations, 19
  see also norm(s)
rejection
  convergence affected by, 48
  of deviants, 44, 46–48, 55, 72
religion in group formation, 37
*Representative Research in
  Social Psychology*,
  Wiesenthal study described
  in, 61n
resistance to change, 72–74

revolutionary leaders, 55
rewards for productivity, 49
rites, 20
  see also norm(s)
rituals, 20
  see also norm(s)
robot technology, 7
rules, 19
  see also norm(s)

safety management, case study
  in, 11–12, 81–87
Saltzstein, H.D., 38
Schachter, S., 50n
scientific management, 2
self-esteem, independence and,
  56, 60
seminars
  composition of, 105–107
  follow-up to, 107
  Grid, 102–103
  implementation resulting
    from, 107
  length of, 104–105
  see also discussion(s)
Sherif, M., 16n, 25, 33n
Skinner, B.F., 14, 15n
slacking-off, case study in,
  10–11, 95–101
Snaniecki, F., 16n
Social Psychology, 33n
social reality
  conformity and, 46
  convergence as fact of,
    111–112
  norms and, 31–32, 40–41
  physical reality vs., 31
socioeconomic level in group
  formation, 37
Sociometry, Sherif study
  described in, 33n

sociotechnical systems, 7
SOP (standard operating
  procedure), 20
  see also norm(s)
Soviet Union, 66–67
spouses as confidants, 58–59
Stagner, R., 16n
standard operating procedure
  (SOP), 20
  see also norm(s)
standards, see norm(s)
Stoffer, S.A., 16n
Strickland, L., 39
structural deviants, 59–60
success
  characteristics of, 65–67
  cohesion brought about by,
    65
  complacency resulting from,
    66–67
suggestion box, 56
supervision
  humanistic, 4
  productivity and, 3–4
  training in, 4
supervisors
  behavior changing tactics of,
    49–50, 73–74
  distrust among, 101
  nonassertive, 96
  norms set by, 8–10
  prevailing norms adopted by,
    74
sweatshops, 2
Synectics: The Development of
  Creative Capacity (Gordon),
  117n

taboos, 20
  see also norm(s)
task leader in discussions, 113

task paragraph, 77–78, 80*n*,
   83–84, 90
Taylor, Frederick W., 2
team building, 107*n*
technical-practical distinction,
   37
tenure, 48
A Theory of Cognitive
   Dissonance (Festinger), 33*n*
Thibault, J.W., 39
Thomas, W.I., 16*n*
thought processes, 111–112
time and motion studies, 2
traditions, 19
   see also norm(s)
training, resistance to, 3

union-management relations,
   case study in, 12–13, 88–94
unions, 2, 4
United States, 66–67, 119

Victims of Groupthink (Janis),
   116*n*

Watson, J.B., 14, 15*n*
welfare state, 4
Wiesenthal, D.L., 61*n*
workers
   psychological testing of, 3
   training of, 3
World War II, 66–67, 119

X, Malcolm, 36